My Brother & I

My Brother & I

C. J. (JONTY) DRIVER

Series Editor: Peter J. Conradi, FRSL

Signed for Martin Pick
with affectionate respect

Jonty
in Norwich 2014

Kingston University Press
SHORT BIOGRAPHY SERIES

Kingston University Press
Kingston University
Penrhyn Road
Kingston-upon-Thames
Surrey, KT1 2EE

Contents © C.J. Driver 2013

British Library Cataloguing in Publication Data available.
ISBN: 978-1-899999-59-0
Published as part of the KUP Short Biography Series.

Series Editor, KUP Short Biography Series:
Peter J. Conradi, FRSL

Set in: Garamond
Typeset by: PK Editorial (www.pkeditorial.co.uk)
Image layout by: PK Editorial (www.pkeditorial.co.uk)

Printed in the UK by Lightning Source

Cover design: Nastasiya Alyakisheva
(nastasiya.alyakisheva@gmail.com)

Cover image: Detail of a painting in oil & pastels by Simon
Driver, of miners crammed in a cage, here reproduced with
permission of the owner, C.J. Driver.

Children of the same family, the same blood, with the same first associations and habits, have some means of enjoyment in their power, which no subsequent connexions can supply; and it must be by a long and unnatural estrangement, by a divorce which no subsequent connexion can justify, if such precious remains of the earliest attachments are ever entirely outlived...

(Jane Austen, *Mansfield Park*)

Acknowledgements

I acknowledge with thanks help given especially by my sister, Professor Dorothy Driver; my brother, Astley Driver; Pat Tucker, meticulous copy-editor and constant friend; and, as ever, my wife, Ann.

A first draft of this essay was written while I held a Fellowship awarded by the Bogliasco Foundation at the Liguria Study Centre in Italy, and I am grateful to the Trustees and the staff for allowing me the leisure to work in luxurious comfort without interruption for four weeks.

An Afterthought on Ampersands

"The ampersand is the last survivor of the almost innumerable contractions used to save labour and material by medieval scribes and early printers. These were discarded, not for aesthetic reasons, but because the extra 'sorts' added to the labour of composition, and to the size and complexity of the trays of type. The ampersand is pleasant to look at and can be extremely useful for economy in a lengthy heading or title, or to make even spacing easier, most of all in narrow measures.

"Some typographers are shy of this decorative and accommodating friend. In nearly forty years' experience of printing in South Africa, I have never had an ampersand substituted when I wanted 'and' to be spelt out; but again and again I have had 'and' printed when I had specified an ampersand. Therefore I am sure that there is no danger of the present generation of printers using the contraction to excess."

(The Rev. Charles Gould, *Author & Printer in South Africa*, 1945)

————

This book is published as part of the Short Biography Series initiated by Kingston University Press to acknowledge innovative works of life-writing, memoir and biography. Further information from KU Press is available at:

www.fass.kingston.ac.uk/kup/short-biography/

About the Author

C.J. Driver (usually called by the diminutive, Jonty – for Jonathan) is a poet, novelist and essayist. For many years a teacher – in Africa, Hong Kong and England - he is now a full-time writer, living with his wife in East Sussex, but travelling regularly to his country of birth, South Africa.

Jonty Driver was born in 1939. After five years at the University of Cape Town, he was elected President of the National Union of South African Students (NUSAS), in 1963 and 1964, and held in solitary confinement by the South African police in 1964 on suspicion of involvement in the African Resistance Movement. While a postgraduate student at Trinity College, Oxford (1965–7), he was refused renewal of his passport and was stateless for five years until becoming a British citizen, although he remained a prohibited immigrant in South Africa until 1991 (apart from one brief visit in 1986). He taught at Sevenoaks School, 1964–5 and 1967–73 (where he was Housemaster of the International Sixth Form Centre); Director, Sixth Form Studies, Matthew Humberstone Comprehensive School in Cleethorpes, 1973–8; Principal, Island School, Hong Kong, 1978–83; Headmaster, Berkhamsted School, 1983–9; and the Master of Wellington College, 1989–2000. He held a research fellowship at the University of York in 1976, and has been an honorary senior lecturer in the School of Literature and Creative Writing at the University of East Anglia since 2007. He was a judge of the Caine Prize for African Writing in 2007 and 2008 and has held residencies at the Liguria Study Centre in Bogliasco, at the MacDowell Colony in New Hampshire, and at the Hawthornden Writers' Retreat.

He has published five novels (the first four of which have recently been re-issued under the imprint, Faber Finds), a biography (of the South African radical, Patrick Duncan) and six books of poetry, the most recent *So Far, Selected Poems 1960–2004*. His *Rhymes for the Grandchildren: Moose, Mouse and Other Rhymes*, was published by the Peridot Press in November 2011. The Happenstance Press is publishing twenty-six of his poems in a pamphlet, *Citizen of Elsewhere*, in 2013.

Also by this author

Novels:
Elegy for a Revolutionary
Send War in Our Time, O Lord
Death of Fathers
A Messiah of the Last Days
Shades of Darkness

Biography:
Patrick Duncan, South African and Pan-African

Poetry:
Occasional Light (with Jack Cope)
I Live Here Now
In the Water-Margins
Holiday Haiku
Requiem
So Far, Selected Poems, 1960–2004
Citizen of Elsewhere

Preface

This is "an essay in biography and some poems", rather than simply a biography and some poems. That isn't just because it is shorter than most biographies – a "brief life" was a tempting title for more than one reason – but "essay" is meant in more than just a technical sense: especially with the sequence of poems as an integral part of the venture, this is an exploration, a testing out, an "essay", an "assay", into a particular relationship, in a particular context, at a particular time - above all else an elegy, but an elegy spoken in a voice which I hope my dead brother Simon would have approved of: quiet, undramatic, level-headed, matter of fact, sensible as well as affectionate. "Don't fuss," he would have said, as our father did.

In fact, the poems came before the prose, though now they follow. At first, each poem arrived singly, and one or two of them were published separately. Then, for a while, I hoped there might turn out to be enough of the poems to make a whole book, or a pamphlet at least. So, nine were published in *So Far, Selected Poems 1960-2004*, as being "*From* Love & Death in Cape Town". In due course, I realised either the impulse had passed or the sequence was as complete as it could be made. Now, they will have to stay as they are, and will I hope be sufficient in themselves, perhaps with the verbal equivalent of a musical structure. They are however not an afterthought to the prose, but a pre-thought, or a set of pre-thoughts.

You may, if you wish, read the poems first, and then the prose; or you may read the poems and ignore the prose, or read the prose and then think, Well, I can't be bothered with that kind of conversational blank verse. As always, I am obedient to Ford Madox Ford's injunction to Ezra Pound, "…nothing that you couldn't in some circumstances, in the stress of some emotion actually say." I hope that, at least, the voice which speaks the prose will be perceived to be the same voice as speaks the poems. In a sense, this is all "life-writing", a term much broader than a mere translation into English of "bio-graphy".

C.J. (Jonty) Driver,
February 2013

• Simon Driver

My Brother & I

An essay and some poems

My brother Simon was born – according to our mother – half an hour before midnight on 31 March 1941. We used to tease him by pretending that she had advanced the official time of his birth so that his birthday wouldn't be treated as a joke on April Fools' Day. Both denied the story. Even so, he was, for sure – as he used to say himself – an odd bloke.

First, he was red-haired, with a particularly vivid variety of redness: not the gentle blondish gingery kind, nor the deep red called auburn, but a fiercely burnished coppery red. I've seen it on very few other people and, when I do, my heart always stutters a moment in remembering him, even though by the time he died there was no red left in his hair, and very little hair either. His colouring meant that he sunburned easily and so was very freckled, especially in what the travel advertisers insisted on calling 'sunny South Africa', even in the worst years of apartheid. I remember once we pretended to him that banana skins would rub out freckles. He knew we were teasing, and that he shouldn't believe us; but later we found him standing in front of his bedroom mirror, rubbing away at the multitudinous freckles with a banana skin.

Secondly, he was born after our father went away to war. I'm not sure I remember much of anyone before the war, except perhaps some large, benevolent not-my-mother male, who used to stand in the bathroom in the mornings, shaving and singing – 'Cherry ripe, cherry ripe, Ripe I cry, Come my pretty one, Come and buy', and 'I am a courtier grave and serious, Who is about to kiss your hand', and something about today being his wedding day – and when I hear those songs I think I might just be able to remember him as he was then; but I might only be remembering when he came back.

Simon hadn't even set eyes on him, and didn't until he was five. Some South African troops fighting in North Africa did get leave to come home every now and then; but (although he wasn't really a soldier, since he was an Anglican priest and never carried weapons, even when his regiment was in battle) he was captured – along with thousands of other Allied troops – in the first great battle of Tobruk, flown across the Mediterranean to a camp in Italy and then, after the Italians surrendered, transported in a cattle truck to Germany.

Before my brother's birth in 1941 we had moved from Cape Town to Kroonstad, a flat, dusty town on the northern edge of the Orange Free State; our mother's father was the Anglican Rector of Kroonstad, and a canon of Bloemfontein Cathedral. It's possible that the large male presence I think I remember playing boisterous games with me on a lawn outside a building (which could only have been the block of flats in a suburb of Cape Town my parents and I had been living in at the time) wasn't my father but one of my mother's brothers, probably Charles, the airman, my godfather, after whom I am named, and who would apparently sit for hours on the verandah with me asleep in a pram beside him, watching over me; or perhaps it was her other brother, Astley, red-haired too, but gingery not coppery like Simon, clever at mathematics, training to be an accountant, who joined the artillery when the war broke out. Or perhaps it's just that I wish I could remember them, not only from their photographs and portraits, and the stories we were told about them.

Neither Charles nor Astley came back from the war. South Africans 'went north' to fight and, when they were killed, they 'went west'. Charles had joined the South African Air Force several years before the war, straight from school; he used to tell his sisters he knew he wouldn't be coming back, and he took a Union Jack in his luggage to cover his coffin. Astley had thought he would come back, but he didn't; he died of wounds in the first big retreat of the desert war, directing fire against Rommel's tanks.

The family heard the story of Charles's death direct from our father, who by then was chaplain of the anti-aircraft regiment stationed in the valley in Abyssinia next to where Charles's squadron was. As a pilot in the regular airforce, Charles was used to test-fly fighter planes after they had been repaired. He had taken a particular plane up three times, but told the mechanics he still wasn't happy with it. They did some more work, and he took it up again; this time it flew straight into a mountainside.

The squadron didn't have its own chaplain, so the commanding officer telephoned the regiment in the next valley to ask if their chaplain could take the funeral for them. 'Of course,' said our father. 'I'll come this afternoon. What's the man's name?'

'Charles Gould' he was told; and so he found himself taking a brother-in-law's funeral. He had known both brothers before he had met their elder sister, because they were small boys in the school of which he became head boy before winning the Rhodes Scholarship which took him to Trinity College, Oxford, for his degree in Divinity. He met Phyllis Gould on the Union Castle liner which was taking him back from Cape Town for the last year of his degree; she was going to England to train as a nurse – a rich aunt from Bath was paying for an impoverished colonial girl to come back 'home' to finish her education with a sensible qualification (she had already given her a year in France to learn the language). When Charles saw who was on board the boat with his sister, he dug her in the ribs;

'That's Jos Driver,' he said: 'you'll be lucky if you meet him.' (Father's Christian names were Kingsley Ernest; but no one except his sisters called him anything but Jos. Indeed, most Driver men were called Jos, except the original John Ogilvie Stanford Driver, who – oddly enough – was always called Jack.) By the end of the voyage to Southampton, Jos and Phyllis were in love and, before she could begin her training as a nurse, he had turned up at her aunt's house to propose. They were engaged for four years before they had enough money to marry.

When Astley was killed, all the family knew was that he had died of wounds on a hospital ship in Tobruk harbour. For many years, we thought that his body had been buried at sea, in the harbour. More recently, I have discovered that he was buried in Tobruk itself, and have been told where the grave is. If my brother were still alive, I think he would want us to visit that grave, now that we know where it is and Libya has changed governance. Astley had been Simon's godfather – and there was always some sort of shadowy balance: Charles and Astley; Charles Jonathan and Simon. It always puzzled us that he wasn't named 'Astley Simon' or 'Simon Astley'; it was our other brother, born well after the war, who was named after Uncle Astley.

In Kroonstad we lived, at first, in the rectory, which stood behind the church, but then our mother's younger sister, Imogen, whose husband, Bill Clymer, had also gone north, came to live in the town too, and the two of them rented a small house with a green corrugated iron roof. Though we lived in the rectory for months only, I remember it much more vividly than I do that house; indeed, I could still draw a map of its rooms and garden, and where the church was, and the servants' quarters, and the two fir trees planted in the back yard to celebrate my birth, then my brother's.

On one side of the house, off a dark passageway, was grandfather's study, every wall lined with books; then came the dining room with the glass on display, and the good silver in drawers with green baize linings; then came our grandparents' bedroom; then the guest rooms (suddenly, I remember Simon and me being made to stand still in one of them, while mother tried out clothes on us; when I got impatient, she told us the story of the emperor's new clothes). On the right of the passage was the sitting room, and then, down a dark step, the kitchen.

There was a path from the garden down to the river, where, most mornings, grandfather would swim. We weren't allowed even to paddle there – the river was deep and muddy, and the banks were steep; grandfather would dive in, swim to the other side and then back again, and then swim a little way up and down the river, while we sat on his towel on the bank.

He kept us close to him, in those years after both his sons had been killed.

Simon and I had a sandpit under a pepper tree, and we used peppercorns to decorate our castles; I can never smell peppercorns without remembering life in the rectory. We used to sit on the arm of grandfather's chair or in his lap and he would let us taste his tea, which he drank, as I still do, weak and with lemon, no milk or sugar. When we showed an interest in the picture books, he taught us to turn pages without tearing them. When we came in from the garden or the river he would wash our hands at the same time as he washed his own, holding them between his and using a soft nailbrush first on our nails, then on his own. His bed was piled high with pillows to prop him up at night, because he suffered from sinusitis; the Orange Free State could be cold in winter, and the rectory was – by South African standards – old and damp.

There was a horrible curate who frightened us by trying to make us step into his cupped hands so that he could lift us on to his shoulders; Simon obliged, but I refused, and the curate locked me in the church. I was more frightened of the curate than of being locked in the church, even in the dark, but there was a huge row with my grandfather and the curate left.

One of the servants died after lighting a coal fire in a bucket in her unventilated room at the back of the rectory; the police came, and an ambulance, and my brother and I were taken for a walk so that we would be out of the way.

A farmer brought in the boot of his car two springbok he had shot. Simon and I wept when we saw the beautiful dead animals being carried to be hung in the larder. Did we eat them later? I suppose we did; in those days one ate what was put in front of one. However, we hated butcher shops, and would make mother cross the road rather than go past one (we discovered a few years later that our father had had exactly the same scruples as a boy).

We hated having our hair cut, too, and, once we got too old for our mother to trim it with nail scissors, it became granddad's job to drag us, protesting, to what we learned to call 'the hairdresser', never 'the barber'. Simon drew a line at having the back of his neck shaved with an electrical clipper, saying he would be sick if the man put it anywhere near him; when the man persisted, Simon showed he meant what he said. From then on both of us always had the last stage of haircutting done with hand-clippers.

Grandfather was a bibliophile and a theologian, who kept what hold he could on an intellectual life by corresponding with old friends in England. One of them was Frederick L. Griggs, who illustrated many of the celebrated series of travel guides to the English counties, *Highway & Byways*, published early in the twentieth century; prints from the series, and two of the original drawings given by Griggs to grandfather, hung in the passageway of the rectory. He wrote a guide to (1912) and then a history of (1924) the Grahamstown Cathedral, where he held his second curacy (his first was in the church of St Mary Redcliffe, in Bristol). He wrote a pamphlet, *Author & Printer in South Africa*, published for the Imprint Society in Johannesburg in 1945 – still thoroughly sound in its good sense; I recently won an argument over the use of the ampersand by quoting what he wrote all those years ago.

He tried to have other books published, too: I still have the typescript of *Everyday Religion, A Collection of Essays*, by Charles Gould, Rector of St George's, Kroonstad, and Canon of Bloemfontein Cathedral, with an introduction by the Dean of Johannesburg and dedicated to Wilbert Howard Philip, Bishop of St Albans, & John, Bishop of Derby, 'friends from the morning till the later hours'. The letter of rejection from the editorial secretary at SPCK House says, 'Rising costs make books more and more expensive; the rise in cost of living makes book buyers more parsimonious. So any hopes we had of trying to publish your book have been extinguished.' Grandfather must have been disappointed; when the essays were first published in a local newspaper they were well received. His notes in copybook script sent with the typescript make it plain he was expecting to be published: they included a request for the 'use of one family of type, preferably old-faced roman, so that the half-title, title-page, page and chapter-headings, small capitals, and italics will harmonize with the text'.

Much of the Africana he had collected was sold on his death, to help provide for his widow. Ten or twelve years later, when it became apparent that my father was never going to have the time to read the theological books, Simon and I helped him pack them up to give to St Paul's theological college in Grahamstown. About the same time, Simon took over the maps and the art books. The poetry came to me: Arnold, Bridges, Brooke, Browning, all the way down the alphabet to William Watson, Walt Whitman and the eight-volume edition of the *Poems of William Wordsworth* by W. Knight. Every now and again, I think I should give to a library some of grandfather's special books – for instance, Gilchrist's *Life of Blake*, with illustrations (taken from the original plates), or a very early edition of Samuel Johnson's *Rasselas*; but then I decide to hang on to them for a few years more.

I remember from those years a nightmare. It must have been before we moved from the rectory. A pile of gravel (or sand or topsoil) had been dumped outside the front gate and we had been told not to climb it. Perhaps we had, nevertheless, and had been ticked off. In my dream, Simon and I were on top of the pile, singing, 'We're the king of the castle', when suddenly the Dirty Rascal, an archetypal Ragged Man – perhaps a version based on one of the 'poor white' tramps who often turned up at rectories seeking succour of some kind, and who would be directed to the back door for a meal or old clothes (anything but money or drink), and who might have frightened my brother and me, or perhaps it was the nasty curate, though I don't remember the reality, just the dream afterwards – was at the base of the pile, snarling, 'No, you're not'. He has then taken our place on top of the pile, and I am holding Simon's hand as we go running down the garden path to the front door of the rectory. I lose hold of his hand, and I can't get the door open, and the Ragged Man is in pursuit, and is about to get first Simon, then me. When in due time I came across the Ragged Man of myth and story, I could give him a face and a body very easily.

Another disconnected memory of those years is of mother's borrowing a homemade rotary sieve from a neighbour so that we could sieve the brown wholemeal flour to get enough white flour to make a sponge cake for Simon's birthday party. Sieving flour was illegal, and the sieve had to be carried from the neighbour's house to ours in the dark, safely wrapped up. Our mother hated borrowing the sieve and breaking the law for fear of being seen as undermining the war effort; but the birthday cake was a special treat.

Our grandmother, with her three Christian names – Maud Gwendolyn Georgiana – came from an upper-class English family but married not someone grand and rich but Charles James Baines Gould, a young clergyman from North Devon farming stock. When I got to understand the English class system better I worked out that some people might have thought she had married 'a little beneath her'; but then I also worked out that she was several years older than Charles Gould, so perhaps there was another reason for marrying. She had been a violinist sufficiently good to have played in a semi-professional orchestra in England, although, by the time we went to live in the rectory, she had stopped playing because of arthritis in her hands; I don't suppose there was much demand for violinists in Kroonstad. When she was a girl, someone in the family had given her the money to buy a special violin made by the Brothers Carcassi in Florence in 1751, and in due course it became mine.

Grandmother had a considerable collection of 78 records, which she played in the evenings on an EMI record-player, one of the early electric models, with a huge papier-mâché horn and no controls, even for volume. To get it going, one turned on the electricity and then spun the turntable until the current took over. The needles were made of bamboo and had to be sharpened after each side was played. Once we had learned how to use the machine, and to sharpen the needles, we were allowed to do so whenever we wanted, and many hours of Simon's and my childhood were spent with our heads tucked almost inside the horn, listening to Kreisler, Gilbert and Sullivan, Beethoven, 'Our Village Concert', Gracie Fields, Bruch, Bruckner, Bach, Paul Robeson, Mendelssohn, Rachmaninoff: not much order or system in that, but we were never a very orderly family in an intellectual sense – too much variety for good order.

Our grandmother's father was Major General Astley Terry and the family had lived in a big house in Berkshire. The house had been sold because her father had run up debts (in pursuit of actresses in London, so the story went, though I'm not sure how one reconciles that with the fact he was a Knight of the Order of St John of Jerusalem; Simon had a photograph of him as an old man looking venerable in his robes of office. This was passed on to me after Simon's death and hangs with other old photographs above the staircase in our tiny English cottage).

Our grandfather's family came from the parish of Charles on the edge of Exmoor. Great-grandfather John Gould had been a Methodist minister sent for five years after the Anglo–Boer War to minister in South Africa – he became 'president of the circuit' there – and, when the family went back to England, grandfather was sent by the Methodists to school in Cambridge and then to the university. While he was there, he had changed back to being an Anglican ('converted' is too strong a word; as he always reminded us, the founders of Methodism had never intended to become a denomination separate from the established church of England). However, whatever his theological reasons had been, he had then been required (and no doubt required it of himself) to repay the Methodists his Cambridge fees from his meagre Anglican salary; 'the debt' was a shadow over the rest of his and grandmother's married life, until there fell the darker shadows of the deaths of both their sons, eighteen months apart.

When we were older, neither Simon nor I remembered hearing of first Charles's death and then Astley's, though we must have been there when the news arrived. Nearly sixty years later, at a memorial service for our younger brother's twenty four year-old son, killed in a car accident, my mother, then in her late eighties and very forgetful, turned to the rest of the family in the chapel at St Andrew's College, Grahamstown, and, her face anguished, said, 'This is terrible; it's just like the war when my brothers were killed.' I do remember our mother's breaking the news of the death of our little friend, Peter Moll, who lived on a farm just outside Kroonstad. He had been playing 'Germans', wearing a tin hat and searching the outbuildings of the farm. He must have climbed up to look into a water-storage tank and then toppled in, presumably knocking himself unconscious, because he drowned in only an inch or two of water. I have a tiny scar on my forehead which he made with a front tooth during a fight we had had on the verandah of the rectory; was that before or after we became best friends?

And suddenly I do remember a telegram arriving at the little house, its being opened on the pavement, and mother and her sister throwing it in the air, and dancing in joy, and making us dance too; was that the news of father's release from prison camp? News of his return? What response would there have been to the other telegrams, those which didn't bring good news? Grief was very silent, in those days, and later too.

******

Mother didn't own a car, though some time during the war grandfather was given one to use in the parish; it had a dicky seat, and Simon and I weren't allowed to ride in it without an adult, because mother was afraid we'd try to climb out while the car was moving. Actually, the most danger we were ever in was when grandfather tried to teach grandmother to drive; she never really understood that, to steer a car, one had to keep at least one hand on the wheel – so, when she wanted to change gear, she would use both hands, even when the car was heading for a *donga* (a deep ditch). Grandmother never did learn to drive, even after grandfather had died and she was living on her own, back in Grahamstown.

Out of the haze comes a memory of my persuading Simon to push a bean up his nose, and being driven to a doctor with him, so that the doctor could hook it out. How can I be sure that I persuaded him to do something so silly, so dangerous? I don't remember persuading him; I do remember being blamed and accepting the responsibility.

Our mother and her sister went almost everywhere in Kroonstad by bicycle; I used to ride on the back of mother's bike, Simon on the back of Imogen's. I remember that once, despite all the instructions to the contrary, he let a leg get caught in the spokes of the back wheel. The bike must have crashed, and Simon's leg was lacerated; they had set off for the rectory a few minutes before us, and we found them by the roadside, the bike in the road, and Imogen and my little brother both in tears, while she dabbed at the cuts and grazes.

Both sisters had trained as auxiliary nurses – Voluntary Aid Detachments (VADs) – and suddenly there comes a memory of how wonderfully professional they looked, in their white uniforms with blue piping; but on that occasion Imogen's professionalism deserted her – she thought she had crippled her sister's second son. She had had a bad accident herself as a girl, when a broken handlebar of a bike had gone right through her upper thigh, scarring it badly. When she was in her bathing costume, and I asked about it, she would tell me it hadn't been nearly as sore as the time she trod in bare feet on a scorpion; she had nearly died then.

Because it was wartime, holidays were rare. Once, we went to stay extravagantly in a hotel in East London; but it was not a pleasant hotel and no sooner had we arrived than we fell ill, one after the other: first aunt, then mother, then me, then brother. We managed only one outing to a beach, and that was cold and damp; we went to a zoo, where we saw crocodiles. I remember a man throwing an empty matchbox into the open jaws of one of the crocodiles. Aunt Imogen (whom Simon and I always called 'Anty') ticked the man off; she was smaller, prettier and even more outspoken than mother; the man said something back, Anty snapped fiercely at him, and we walked away. In later years, whenever we wanted to comment on a holiday, we would say, 'Well, at least it wasn't as bad as East London'.

There was however one wonderful holiday, somewhere in the Eastern Cape. I'm not sure which town it was we visited – Ladysmith, perhaps, or Queenstown (grandfather had at one stage been a minister in a poor area of Port Elizabeth, and then rector of Cradock, so that side of the family knew the Eastern Cape well, though perhaps not as well as the Drivers) – but we went there by train to stay with friends who had a large, low-slung bungalow with wooden verandahs on three sides and a long, green and overgrown garden. I remembered the house and garden so well, and where it stood in relation to the railway line which ran nearby, and the road over the railway line into the *koppies* (hills), that, years later, I surprised mother by drawing a map of house, road and railway line which she said was exactly as she remembered the area, too.

It was on that holiday I had my first conscious apprehension of the beautiful. First, the family we stayed with had a record of a treble singing 'Jesu, Joy of Man's Desiring'. I must have been playing in the garden with Simon when I first heard the record, and I remember running up from the garden, transfixed by what I had heard, and asking for it to be played again.

Then there was, on the sides of the *koppies* just outside town, an extraordinary display of flowering aloes, red and yellow, even more vivid because of the dry and stony Karoo landscape as background; every day, mother would wheel Simon in his pram, with me safely in tow, up over the railway line and on to the dusty road through the *koppies*, so we could look at the aloes. I work out now that I was still only four years old when we took that brief holiday. I know Simon remembered the holiday as vividly as I do, because it was one of the things we talked about when he was dying.

******

• The Family before Simon

Back row left to right: Charles Gould, "Jos" Driver, Imogen Clymer ("Anty"), Astley Gould

Front row left to right: Maud Gould, Jonty (as a baby), the Reverend Charles Gould, Phyllis Driver

• Simon at work

• Simon & his big brother

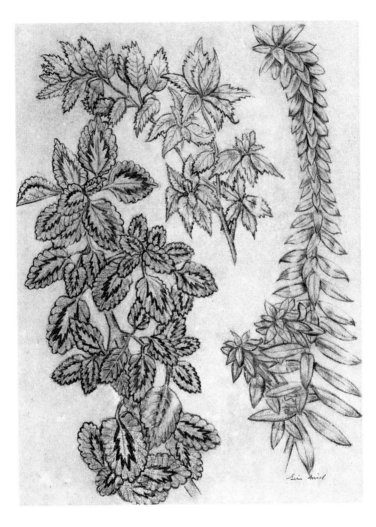

• Simon Driver: a late drawing

Because mother was concerned that I would forget my father – and because Simon had never even seen him – we were made to kiss a photograph of him every night as we were going to bed. We knew he was a prisoner of war, but it was hard to connect him with the other prisoners of war whom we saw in town. Kroonstad Gaol was used to house Italian POWs; most of them were paroled and would walk around the streets in groups, dressed in blue overalls. Simon and I liked them because they made much of any children they saw; no doubt they flirted with the mothers too. I remember my mother pushing Simon's pram across to the other side of the road to avoid a group of prisoners and seem to remember being confused by her explanation: they were the enemy, but we had to be kind to them, because father was their prisoner too, and we wanted them to be kind to him, but they were still the enemy.

There were Royal Air Force airmen in Kroonstad too; they had a training camp there. One of them, a pilot called Ralph (pronounced Rafe), made friends with mother and her sister, and would come to tea, at home or in the rectory. The two young women (as I now realise they were) went dancing with him, but always together, so there could be no gossip. After the war, he kept in touch a little, with letters at Christmas time, until he was shot down and killed in the Korean War. I think there was a time when I might have wondered if he was our father, though sometimes I thought that about granddad too. Certainly, I knew that grandfather was as good as other people's fathers. He had been in the first war, in action in East Africa, although, as a clergyman, he too hadn't carried weapons (as often as not, he would call himself 'a clerk in holy orders' rather than a 'priest' or a 'clergyman', and never, I think, a 'minister'). He did however have a pair of binoculars (though he taught me to call them field glasses, just as my grandmother didn't like us to talk about mirrors; they were looking glasses). They were Zeiss, made in 1917, and he had found them in a tent belonging to a German officer who had managed to get clear, just before the South African forces arrived, though he had had to leave all his possessions behind.

One day, without grandfather's permission, I borrowed the field glasses to show them off to some other small boys I played with in the park below the rectory. As I had been taught, I kept them around my neck so they couldn't be dropped; but the leather strap broke, and I put them back in his study, desperately worried about what he would say. In the end, I confessed; so he took out a penknife and cut the strap a little shorter, and made a new hole, and no harm was done.

Most white people in Kroonstad were Afrikaners and many of them were Afrikaner nationalists too. The Molls, parents of my friend Peter, were relatively rare in the Free State in being both Afrikaners and supporters of the United Party – the old South African

Party – and its leader, General Smuts. Simon and I weren't even aware that we spoke Afrikaans as easily as we spoke English until the episode of the field glasses; one of the little boys asked me what they were, and without thinking I gave the Afrikaans name, 'verkykers' (literally, far-lookers). We must have spoken some Sesotho too, though not a word of that remains on my tongue or in my brain; not only were there black servants in the rectory but on the Molls' farm we played with black children; and in the town – and especially in the rough park near the rectory – there was a gang of little black boys with whom we usually had a war. We would fight with sticks. One of the black boys found a forked stick, and became adroit at using it to wrest our sticks away from us; he would catch his opponent's stick in the fork, twist suddenly, and it would fly out of one's hands, almost as if by magic.

Years later, when I was working for the National Union of South African Students, I made friends with Asha Ntanga, a black law student at the University of Natal in Durban. He was a big flamboyant man, rugby-playing, womanising, hard-drinking. When we were talking one evening about our upbringing, he mentioned that he had grown up in Kroonstad. We were almost the same age. Had he been in a gang, I asked? Had they fought a gang of white boys with sticks? Did he remember a boy who had had a forked stick which he used to twist the white boys' sticks out of their hands? Yes, said Asha, suddenly a little grim; some white bastard had crashed his stick down into the fork, and the magic stick had split into two. I confessed to Asha that the miscreant was me, but we also remembered that, after the fight, some of the black boys had come round to our mother's house and she had given them lemonade and cakes – but not, of course, in the kitchen: out in the back yard.

Officially, apartheid came into being only after 1948; but it had existed for years before then, sometimes written down as regulation or even law, sometimes merely acknowledged as custom. To separate the prejudice of class from the prejudice of race would, I think, require a Solomon. Many white South Africans of liberal or left-wing persuasion could recount the story of when 'the scales fell from their eyes' and they became non-racist; the Pauline image was commonly used. However, as far as I can tell, Simon and I were never racists, and I account for that mainly because, often on a Sunday morning, our grandparents would have one or another local black clergyman and his wife to breakfast. We were expected to treat them exactly as we would any other visitor.

The Christianity went deeper than that; while neither grandfather nor father was a missionary, the missionary impulse was still powerful in our family. In the church hall where we went for Sunday school, one of the paintings on the wall showed Jesus surrounded by a group of children of all races, black, white, brown, yellow; it caught my imagination so much that, when we moved to Grahamstown after the war, I asked if I could have the picture. My parents thought I meant another picture which hung in the hall – of Jesus knocking at the door of the human heart where the door has no outside handle – but I didn't like that. I wanted the one of Jesus with all the children. Mawkish it may be – the children are all very clean in their national costumes and all good-looking, and Jesus is a brown-blond Gentile, not a Palestinian – but it was not without a point many long and bitter years before South Africa became a 'rainbow nation'.

When the POW camp in which our father was held was liberated by American soldiers, there was, of course, nowhere for the prisoners to go – or, rather, no way of getting there, except by walking, which some apparently started to do. Our father was in no fit state to walk anywhere; the years of captivity had weakened him desperately. Moreover, the life-saving Red Cross parcels sent to prisoners contained cigarettes as well as food and clothes. Since his school days he had been a heavy smoker. There are photographs of him at school relaxing with friends, and even then he sometimes had a pipe in his mouth. In prison camp he swapped the food from his parcel for tobacco. He was six foot three and strongly built, a second-row forward in rugby parlance; his healthy weight was sixteen stone, but by the end of the war he weighed less than eight stone. When eventually he got to England, he had to spend six months in a Brighton hospital recovering. Then he went to our great-aunt in Bath for more recuperation. She – who when he had first arrived from Oxford to propose to her niece had kept him waiting outside the front door while she found out what was going on – had every night for all the months since he had been freed put a hot water bottle in the bed she had had made up for him, ready for his arrival.

More months of waiting followed: for a place on a ship to take him back to Cape Town, for a seat on the troop train for the long journey northwards to the Orange Free State, and Kroonstad. We didn't even know for sure he was on the train until he managed to get to a telephone in Bloemfontein station to let us know he would be arriving at midnight.

Grandmother stayed at home in the rectory; the arrival of the troop train carrying so many people she knew, but not the two she loved most, would have been too much for her to bear; but grandfather drove mother, Anty, Simon and me to the station to wait. Mother held Simon in her arms, for he was a little shaky from being woken; I stood next to her, trying to be grown-up, nearly seven, already tall for my age. As the train arrived, huffing and puffing up the platform, men in uniform or in civilian suits began to pile out of the doors from the crowded corridors, some squeezing out of windows in their haste. Then we saw the man whose photograph we had kissed, taller by a head than most men on the platform, and seemingly even taller because of the cap his rank entitled him to, slowly pushing his way through the crowds towards us. As he came up to us, Simon turned to our mother to say, 'Is that my real Daddy?' When she said it was, he held out his arms to be taken.

I have always thought of that moment of return and recognition as in some ways the beginning of Simon's and my real lives, as if what had happened before then wasn't quite true – just a set of stories, which happened to some children a bit like us, but which didn't have any great significance. I have always found those moments of return and recognition between a parent and a child, or between a husband and a long-lost wife, the most intensely moving episodes in all literature. Imagine what it would have been like for my brother and me if that tall man in uniform who came smiling through the crowd on the station towards us had not been our father after all. If he had walked straight past us to some other family on the platform – we were not the only people there waiting for the return of a soldier from the war. Or if he had not arrived at all – if it was all just a story. And now that I am older, my father long since dead and my own sons grown up and with their own children at the age I was then, I think back to what it must have been like for our grandfather, waiting on the platform for his son-in-law to come home, when his own sons would never return. All my life, and during my brother's much shorter life, we were conscious that we were living the lives our uncles hadn't had.

******

Despite the wonder of that moment, it wasn't an easy homecoming. Years later, mother confessed to me that father had been so brutalised by his experiences in POW camp that she had, at one stage, threatened to take Simon and me and leave him. He was very fierce with us: if we were disobedient, or rude, or misbehaved, we were taken upstairs to our rooms, bent over and spanked, quite fiercely, with a slipper or hairbrush – later, several times, he used a proper cane on my backside.

That wasn't the hardest thing to take: Simon and I had got used to having our mother to ourselves. We were the centre of her life and we had her younger sister, 'Anty', married herself to a soldier, but without children until after the war, so always there to help. It was almost like having two mothers. Now Anty wasn't living with us any more and, quite suddenly, our mother had ceased to be simply that, and became first and foremost our father's wife; we had to learn that, in everything, we came second to him. She was his wife, and only after that was she our mother.

In many ways, it was good for us. For instance, we were never able to play one parent off against the other. If we asked him whether we might do something, the reply was always, 'Ask your mother'. She would tell us to ask our father.

'But he told us to ask you', we would say.

'Then you will have to wait until we have talked to each other.'

'But then it will be too late.'

'And you will learn to be patient.'

When, in due time, I came to read D.H.Lawrence's *The Rainbow*, I knew precisely what he meant by the image of the child's growing up in the safety of the arch of the parents' marriage. In the meantime, we had to learn new ways; the morning after his return I wandered sleepily into my mother's bedroom, expecting as usual to snuggle into the warmth next to her, only to find this large stranger there already. 'How long is he going to stay?' I asked.

The father's return meant that the brothers became even closer than we had been, especially when Anty left Kroonstad to live in Bloemfontein with her husband. Of course, grandparents were still there; but in some strange way extended family narrowed down into nuclear family and, in doing so, made feelings more complicated, rather than simplifying them. Moreover, I was the first-born, the big brother, always a bit stronger, much taller, a bit quicker, despite my tendency to illness, sooner to speak, sooner to decide. Simon came very slowly to language, partly I guess because I was always there to say for him what he might have said himself. 'Why is Simon crying?' our mother would ask.

'He fell down and hurt his knee,' I would answer – and for years thought that was what I was meant to do. For a time, my mother had wondered if he might actually be a little slow mentally, because when he might have spoken he always looked to me to speak for him. Then, suddenly one day (I think he was actually three), he started to speak – and his first words were a complete sentence. He had had his tonsils removed and, as he came round from the anaesthetic, he signalled to the nurse at his bedside that he wanted something to drink. She gave him unsweetened orange juice and it burned his throat. 'I think you're horrible,' he said to her, handing the glass back. The nurse was upset, and told my mother.

'He's never spoken like that before,' my mother replied. 'That's his first sentence.' I suspect the nurse thought mother was trying to excuse a rude child; but it was true. He hadn't needed to speak until then – and all his life he stayed laconic, both in speech and in writing.

Part of the reason was that he was a classic dyslexic, from his earliest days strongly left-handed in a right-handed world. Whenever he was under pressure, he would write from the right hand side of the page to the left; when he became a commercial artist, the one thing he hated doing was free-hand lettering, which required him to work from left to right across the page. No matter how carefully he worked, even with his left hand twisted round so that he seemed to be writing upside down, something would always get smudged by his wrist or his arm or his sleeve. Letters like 'd's and 'b's were regularly interchanged, 'c's and 'e's back to front, and the sequencing of letters in words was likely to vary every time he used them, sometimes within a line or two. His defence against the teachers who scrawled corrections (in those days, often in red ink) across even his most careful work was to write as little as possible, and to use no words he wasn't absolutely sure how to spell. I found recently a letter he sent me in June 1967 in England to congratulate me on my impending marriage. 'Dear Jonty', he wrote,

> I am very happy that you are getting married. The whole family is very excited about it. Mommy says it's the first wonderful thing that has happened to her for years. She is very excited about seeing you again.
> I wrote to her and told her that I hoped she would go when I first heard the news, but I think she had already made up her mind to go.

What are your plans? I know that you and Ann are going to Sevenoaks in September. Have you decided anything about the future, if you will stay in England. With your Oxford degree you can get a job anywhere.

Dorothy [our sister] and I are both sorry that we will not be there on the 8th but we will be thinking about you. I think that Dorothy will come to England in March of next year. She has got a very good job, earning good money.

The two of us are planning to get a flat together in October or November, in Seapoint or Bantry Bay if we can find something reasonable. I don't know how it will work out as we are both very [stubbo(rn) crossed out] independant (sic) and like our own way.

I am at present living in a hotel in Sea Point, much more reasonable than the boarding house I was in before and I am having quite a good time here.

I am still in the same job and have had a very reasonable increase. They are sending me to Durban next week for a few days so that should be quite pleasant.

I will be writing again in a few days time, but this is just to wish you all the happiness in your marriage.

Yours, *Simon*

If I had teased him about how matter-of-fact he sounded, even when I knew he was deep-down delighted, he would have said, 'Well, I knew you would know what I meant.' He wrote much as he talked, always in short and simple sentences, using as few subordinate clauses as he could. In language as in everything else, he hated what he called 'fuss' or 'showing off' – and he was quite right that I would know what he meant, even when he hadn't said it. I remember once, when he came to visit me in Oxford, someone commented on the fact that we had been sitting in the same room for some time, without talking. 'Have you had a row, or something, that you aren't talking to each other?'

'We don't need to talk to each other,' Simon answered. 'We know what we are thinking.'

And I think we did, about most of the things which mattered. We felt the same about the same sort of people. If one of us liked someone, we knew the other would too. If one of us was pretending to feel something that we didn't really feel, the other would spot the falsity, too. Nothing needed to be said: half a gesture, the slightest glance, a hesitation, a silence, would reveal to the other what was felt. I wish I could remember more of what he actually said; but it wasn't so much the words themselves as his manner of saying them, the askance glance, the oblique retort, the quiet aside: never designed to hurt nor to give offence, but so often vivid in its intriguing oddity.

******

We didn't stay long in Kroonstad after our father came back. Very quickly, he found a post back at his old school, St Andrew's College in Grahamstown, as chaplain and teacher of Classics and Divinity. Grahamstown was the original main settlement of the British sent out in 1820 to try to keep the peace between the Boers moving up to escape the influence of British imperialism and the black tribes pushing down the coast, or that is what we were taught as youngsters. A hundred and twenty-five years later, it was still in some ways a frontier town; for instance, the main streets were wide enough to turn a wagon with a full span of oxen, and one could visit on the hills around the city the fortified signal-towers which had once been used to let the townspeople know of impending attacks across the colonial borders. The most famous landmark in those days was the copse of pine trees at Makana's Kop above the black township, over which Makana had led his amaXhosa tribesmen in an attack in 1852, apparently after they had been told the white men's bullets would be magically turned to water.

There wasn't enough water in and around the modern Grahamstown to support many industries (especially as the hillsides around the basin in which the town had been built were in those days densely covered with imported wattles and blue gums, which soaked up any water flowing to the stream that had attracted the original settlement). The City Council didn't think industry was appropriate in a city the main purpose of which was education; Grahamstown might look like a small town, but the cathedral made it a city. The result was large-scale black unemployment, especially of the men, and the black township was dreadfully poor.

I have absolutely no memory of the move from Kroonstad. School housing wasn't easily available in Grahamstown after the war, with so many soldiers coming home, so we were put to live in a low, cool, white-painted house, its large garden shaded with trees, in the grounds of St Paul's theological college; we shared the house with Bill Burnett (afterwards Bishop of Bloemfontein and later Archbishop of Cape Town) and his wife, who, when my sister was born in 1948, became her godmother. Bill Burnett was then still training to be a priest; he had been a prisoner-of-war in Italy, like my father, but when the Italians surrendered he had gone into the mountains, and had stayed there for months, living mainly (I understood) on grass. He was spectacularly thin, even by my own skinny standards, but when I commented I was told it was because he had been a brilliant squash player, and squash players were always thin. There were also some young boarders from St Andrews in the house for whom father acted as housemaster; I was forbidden to go into their dormitory, though when my parents were out Simon and I would often go in to play with them. One Sunday morning, when my parents were at church, I went in; the boys were teasing me, so I seized a golf-club from one of them, and pretended to attack him. When I raised the club above my head, it broke a light-bulb. When my parents came back, the misdemeanour was discovered and I was beaten.

Our father's own father had been a magistrate, first on Robben Island (though I have never been able to discover why Robben Island needed a magistrate in 1912; I know it was 1912 because that was the year of our father's birth, and his birth certificate says, clearly, 'Robben Island') and then in Mosselbaai. During the First World War, he had joined the South African forces fighting for Britain and its Empire (as a private, not an officer, despite his being a magistrate, apparently 'to set a good example to the other young men'). Sent to the Western front, he had been killed within a fortnight of his arrival, when his regiment was sent down a sunken road straight into German machine-guns – an action which even the official history of the 1st Regiment South African Infantry describes as 'lamentable'. Private Harry Thackwray Driver 10054 is buried in Brown's Copse Cemetery, near a village in Northern France called Fampoux, near Arras, along with 1,933 British soldiers, 129 other South Africans and two Canadians. His widow, Aurelia Alice, was left to bring up their five children, not on a magistrate's pension but on a private's. Our father, the fourth of those children, must have been five when his father was killed, though for some reason I cannot fathom he used always to say it happened when he was seven; it's only now I check the dates I realise the error.

I think it may be in part a consequence of losing his own father so young that our father was not in conventional terms a particularly good one; he simply didn't know what a father should do with his children. Moreover, he was always busy. He spent very little time with us, whether reading to us, or playing with us, or taking us out. Those were mother's functions. Father had other work to do. That wasn't entirely his fault: as well as being a busy schoolmaster with a full share of teaching, games coaching (he coached both rugby and cricket) and house-mastering, he was a priest and, all our childhood, Saturday nights were sermon-writing nights, not going-out nights, and Sundays were services; in those days, normally three: communion, matins, evensong. I have never really got hold of the concept of 'the weekend'.

Our father had other idiosyncrasies, too, which our mother accommodated: for instance, he didn't much like picnics, particularly at the seaside ('I've had enough sand in my food to last me for ever,' he would say) and he refused to camp. For the rest of his life, he said, he was going to take all his clothes off at least once every day and cover himself with soap and hot water before putting on clean clothes; he'd had more than his share of being unwashed. I can remember only once his coming on a picnic with us in Grahamstown – and to the end of my days the smell of pine needles will remind me of the family walking up to one of the stony hills above the Cradock road and my mother laying a rug for the picnic in a patch of sun among the pine trees. Why did he come with us that day? Was it mother's birthday? It might well have been in July, because it was a cold day, except in the sun. Oddly enough, the fact that he didn't often do things with us made those occasions when he did seem particularly memorable.

We didn't have a car in the years we lived in Grahamstown. Very occasionally, during the school holidays, we would walk to the railway station to catch the early morning train which puffed its way slowly and carefully (the line crossed Blaauwkrantz Gorge, where once the high bridge had collapsed under the weight of the train and many had been killed) forty miles down to where the Kowie River ran into the sea at the little settlement of Port Alfred. We would walk from the station to the river mouth, and then to the lagoon or on to the beach, sometimes as far as Shelly Beach at the far end of the bay, spend the day there, and then catch the train back in the evening: weary, sunburnt, happy.

Once, a few years later, we were lent a house there; it was the extension of a hotel run by a family which sent their boys to St Andrews, but the house was dangerously close to the river's edge and my mother was sure Simon would fall in if the door leading outside was opened. For a reason I can't remember (was there one?) I had a fight with the second son of the owners of the hotel; he pinned me to the lawn outside the hotel, sitting on my chest and grinding my skinny biceps painfully with his knees. Suddenly, I managed to get a hand free, and hit him on the nose hard enough to make it bleed. My brother was very proud of me for that.

Better was being lent the seaside cottage belonging to the headmaster of St Andrew's, Ronald Curry, out on the edge of the Port Alfred golf course. I remember that holiday mainly because I discovered a shelf full of the novels of P.G.Wodehouse, and read them with increasing delight. Wodehouse was then still under a dark cloud of moral disapprobation because he had broadcast from Nazi-occupied France and I had an argument with my father because I said I thought his books were very funny, even if he had behaved badly in the war.

Strangely enough, on the same shelves there was a biography of William Joyce, 'Lord Haw-Haw', executed as a traitor because he had broadcast for the Nazis; I read that too, and decided P.G.Wodehouse must have been different, whatever my father said. No one that funny could be bad.

Nearby, a big new and ugly house – modelled on a Swiss chalet, our parents said – was the holiday home of the Ainslie family. Mr Ainslie was a wealthy auctioneer in Grahamstown; the daughters were a year or two older than me, the brother a year or two younger, the same age as Simon. There must have been a shortage of eligible young men on that holiday, because, while Simon played with their brother, the Ainslie sisters took me riding with them almost every day, galloping down the sandy lanes to the beach, and I fell wordlessly in love with both of the sisters in their fawn jodhpurs and white polo shirts. (It couldn't have been many months later that poor Mr Ainslie went bankrupt; rather than face his creditors, he killed himself and the rich Ainslies were suddenly nearly as poor as the Drivers.)

The best holidays of all, usually after Christmas, sometimes after Easter, were when our parents managed to rent from the Grahamstown diocese for next to nothing (which meant there was always a queue of impoverished clerical families wanting it) the 'clergy cottage' at Bushman's River Mouth. Our mother would hire a truck to take us, our bedding, suitcases, the pots, pans, cake-tins of home-made biscuits and nourishing fruitcake, our father's fishing rods (both those home-made out of bamboo and an expensive fibre-glass one a friend had given him), books, packs of cards for the evenings, a Monopoly set, down the dusty unmade roads to the coast. Mother would ride in the front with the two younger children while father, Simon and I would loll on mattresses in the back of the lorry. All of us and our belongings would be set down outside the clergy cottage, and the lorry would go off again until the day came for us to be collected for the return journey. Sometimes we were able to stay for a whole month in the summer.

The cottage was only a couple of minutes from what was in those days (before the building of a bridge for the coastal road caused a silting-up of sand-banks) a wide lagoon, deep and broad enough to sail on, but mainly shallow enough to be safe, provided one stayed away from the actual mouth of the river, which was full of rocks and dangerous cross- and under-currents. Sometimes my father was able to borrow a heavy little clinker-built rowing-boat; and, when I was nine, I used some of what I had saved in the Post Office (a savings account opened for me by Uncle Charles, and therefore to be used only for Very Special Purposes) to buy from a boy a couple of years older than me, Wally Kitcat, the son of another clergyman, a seven-foot dinghy he had made himself of wooden struts covered with canvas, light enough for me to carry on my back down to and up from the beach (and far too precious to be left there overnight). It had a simple, longboat style sail, though no centreboard; and the oars were not round, but flat, swivelling not in rowlocks but on upright bolts, so one couldn't feather the blades. Because it was made of canvas, one had to watch out for snags and sharp rocks; but it was so light that, once or twice when I did hole it on an expedition upriver, I got back safely by sitting right in the stern or in the bows, with the holed end high out of the water, though Simon had to run along the bank of the river because I couldn't manage him in the boat too, without water flooding in. Then we would repair the hole with a canvas patch and special paint of the kind usually used for repairing roofs, and wait impatiently for it to dry so that we could go back on the river.

******

Our brotherly closeness was compounded when, in 1953, our father decided to leave St Andrew's – taking our mother, sister Dorothy and little brother Astley with him – to be headmaster of Uplands, a prep school in White River, in the Eastern Transvaal, two thousand miles away. Having been day boys in St Andrew's prep school, we were to become boarders for the rest of our schooldays. In some ways, that also meant a greater separation between Simon and me; we had, throughout our childhood, shared a bedroom and now we had to go into dormitories full of strangers. At first, he stayed in the prep school; I had already spent my first year in the senior school. Once or twice a week, I would wander up to his boarding house in the hope of seeing him (he was governed by stricter rules involving bounds than I was); and every Sunday we would meet at our grandmother's cottage on the other side of town. Then, when he was thirteen, he came into Upper, the boarding house into which all the Drivers were always put.

Though the age difference between us was only eighteen months, at school we were two years apart, because I was said to be clever and he was meant to be 'rather thick'. He wasn't in the slightest; but he wasn't good at school work, because both reading and writing were painful to him, and anything which involved sequencing was difficult. Nearly all forms of Maths were a nightmare, though he was quick with money and all calculations to do with money (dyslexics often are, perhaps because learning about money is reinforced by the tactile side of actually handling it).

Very early on, soon after Simon started talking, he claimed he had been in China before he was born. Why this had got into his imagination no one ever knew. He told our mother and me once that the reason he had been slow to speak was that he thought in Chinese, not in English. The only physical evidence he could offer was that the eyes of the Driver family are supposed to be a little 'slitty' – though the red hair that was Simon's most manifest characteristic is unknown among the Chinese. Is it conceivable someone might have told him that there is an unusual degree of ambidexterity in the Chinese – although, if he had been Chinese, his left-handedness would have been just as much of a problem when it came to writing. Had he seen ideograms in a painting and thought that, because Chinese script runs down the page, character by character, it might be easier to write? If he had claimed to be an Arab, that might have made more sense. Yet, however we teased him, he remained adamant: he had come from China.

Not of much use in book-learning, and not merely hopelessly unathletic but actually not interested in competitive games at all, in a culture which placed prowess in games, especially tough games like rugby, at the pinnacle of what was desirable in boys and young men, he found almost nothing to enjoy at school, except the company of a few friends and his art classes. He was good at drawing and he loved painting; the only place in the school where he was happy was the art room, in those days a single classroom, generally available only in lesson-time. Art was not considered a significant subject; it was offered only to those who weren't much good at anything else. By the time Simon came to senior school, even though I wasn't the oldest of the Drivers there – we had two cousins of the same surname in the same house – I was established as a person, big enough to look after myself, admittedly not very good at games, but capable of getting into lowly teams, generally near the top of the class academically, a bit of a lad in terms of rule-breaking – above all else, strong enough to look after my little brother, and with enough friends to summon if numbers were required.

It turned out that the first defence he needed was not so much against other boys as against a master. The first essay (we called them 'compositions' then) required of Simon in the senior school he wrote from right to left, in mirror script, with the occasional misspelling of course, but perfectly understandable. Underneath this essay, the teacher – a man who had taught me in my first year and for whom I had little regard, intellectually or otherwise – had written in red ink, 'Dim-witted'. Furious and indignant, I went to his classroom with my brother's exercise book in my hands. 'It isn't my brother who is dim-witted,' I said. Quite properly, I was sent to my housemaster for rudeness – and in those days that meant I was beaten. I didn't care very much; I had done what I had to do.

Did I over-protect Simon? I have to face the fact that, once we lived apart and especially after I had left South Africa, he learned very quickly to stand on his own feet. Almost certainly it would have been better for him in the long run if I had left him alone earlier, if I had been less prone to swoop down on anyone I perceived as giving him a hard time. At school, he had friends of his own, especially two in the same house, Wingfield and Basson, and Basson was thickset, very strong and quite capable of defending Simon's gentleness and kindness; the thugs of the school distressed him less by their physical bullying than by their cruelty towards everyone and everything. It didn't help that his temper was short and that, although his speeches were brief, his tongue could be very sharp and the accuracy of his comments unerring. Instead of turning away wrath with soft answers, he would fire in a dart: 'The spot on your forehead's burst,' he would tell an acne-ridden bully, or 'Your breath smells'. He was always good at physical repugnance, my little brother.

Perhaps the most celebrated example of this in the family was when I brought home for the holidays a girl-friend whose name was Rosemary and nickname Rosebud. He looked at her carefully, and later – when she was out of hearing – murmured aloud, 'Rosebud, Rosebud…Rosemary, Rosemary…Rather overblown Rose, I'd say.' The pointedness of the comment was so devastating that I fear it spelled the end of my relationship with the girl; if she wasn't that already, she was clearly going to become it all too soon. Was it a cruel remark? Perhaps. My sister has told me that she has always hated this story, and I can see why; but I don't want to pretend Simon was saintly.

******

Simon and I were a long way away from our new home. In those days, pupils at boarding school tended to travel by train, rather than by car or aeroplane. From Grahamstown to White River involved a train journey of three nights and two days, though one of the days was spent in wicked, exciting Johannesburg waiting for the connecting train to take us, overnight, down to Nelspruit on the line to Mozambique, where our parents would collect us in the Uplands School minibus to take us back to White River.

Telephone calls were difficult and expensive, therefore reserved for emergencies. Letters from home were important. Our mother was punctilious about writing; every week, almost without fail, we would have a warm, chatty, inconsequential letter from her, in her sprawling, carelessly elaborate handwriting, detailing what the family had done, how father was, what was happening at Uplands, which parties they had been to. On one occasion, after Simon had joined me at St Andrews, we got home to find out some exciting bit of gossip we thought we hadn't heard. 'But I did tell you,' our mother exclaimed. 'I put it in a letter.'

'Oh, we never read that stuff,' Simon said.

It wasn't fair, but it was, in a way, true. We skimmed through mother's letters, because each tended to be like the last. They were news updates, rather than considered reflections. Our father's letters were much more occasional; sometimes we would get only one in a whole term, but their very irregularity made them seem special. A letter to one of us from father was an event – the letter would be read several times, and kept. With our mother's letters, one reading sufficed and the letter could be discarded.

For all his sharpness of comment, and at the risk of sentimentalising him (because no doubt he could be as cruel as most children) I think Simon must have been born soft-hearted. One of my earliest memories (when we were still living in the rectory, when he could have been no more than three) is of his collecting some earthworms which he found in a puddle and putting them in my grandmother's bed. Her screams when she found the poor creatures – they had tried to escape and had spread themselves over her sheets and pillowcases – still echo in my imagination. I was of course in trouble, because it was assumed I had done the deed out of naughtiness. 'But it wasn't me, it really wasn't,' I cried.

'It was me,' said Simon, unfailingly honest. 'It was raining and they were cold.'

He was forgiven, though I was told firmly I should have stopped him. How could I, when he hadn't told me what he was doing? But of course I should have stopped him; that was what the big brother was there for.

I remember, too, an incident when we were still in the junior classes of the Diocesan School for Girls (yes, for girls; we were always proud to be old boys of a girls' school – the boys' prep school didn't take pupils until they were eight). Simon's class had a new teacher, fresh out of teacher training college, a young woman with long, shining, auburn hair; she leaned over Simon to help him with some work he was trying to do. Instead of listening, he – absent-mindedly – began to stroke the abundant hair falling near his face. 'Lovely hot water bottle', he murmured as he stroked. Children near him began to laugh, and the teacher was cross. So Simon ran away. Someone summoned me from my classroom. 'Your brother's run away', I was told. 'Go and find him'. I ran after him but, when I found him, we decided to keep going until we got home. I don't remember what happened then; I expect mother sent us straight back to school again. At supper that evening, we laughed about what had happened; and my father said that of course Simon had been quite right: it really was a lovely hot water bottle.

******

For some reason, I can't easily fit into the chronology of this essay (which is as much memoir as biography, I suppose) the story of the miserable holiday Simon and

I spent with a cousin, Hilliard, and his family, on the outskirts of what was then the new mining town of Welkom in the Orange Free State. I'm not even sure why we went on the holiday at all; was it because Hilliard's children (Adrian, Driver *major* at school, and his sister, Gail) needed companionship in the hellhole their father had gone to work in? Was it that my father wanted us to have more connection with the wider family? There was an extraordinary physical resemblance between my father and Hilliard; while Hilliard wasn't quite as big as my father (he was sometimes nicknamed 'Little Jos'), there was no mistaking their family connection: the same broad forehead, wide–spaced eyes, high cheek bones, solid jaw, cleft chin, made one think they would be alike in other ways, too. Whatever the reason for sending us on that holiday, it was a mistake, though it did play a significant role in our political education.

Hilliard Driver was the manager of one of the collection points for the Witwatersrand Native Labour Association (the WNLA) near Welkom, not far from where we had spent the war years. The place was a few miles outside the town in a recently built company village which included some dormitories for the newly recruited black miners who came, I guess, from all over Southern Africa, but particularly from the neighbouring protectorate of Basutoland (later to become Lesotho); a medical centre where the miners were processed and examined; showers and clothing stores, though not, as far as I remember, any actual training facilities at all. It was a way-station in the inhuman cycle of migrant labour on which the gold-mining system depended, whereby men were brought from the 'native areas' to the mine compounds to work, often in considerable danger, miles underground for minute wages, before being sent back to the 'reserves', sometimes having accumulated goods and saved money, but often diseased or damaged. Uncle Hilliard (we called him that, though he was a cousin) was clearly proud of the place and its efficiency. Simon and I knew, without needing to tell each other, that there was something utterly dreadful about it.

We (Adrian, Simon and I, though not Gail) were allowed to peer through an inspection window at the crowd of black men lined up, all stark naked, not all of them young, some of them trying desperately to cover their genitals with their hands, before being herded by supervisors into showers like beasts into a dip of disinfectant. Coming as we did from a world of boys' boarding schools, Simon and I weren't shy of naked bodies, nor unaware of male genitals and their variety – but when we were on our own, later, we agreed that for boys like us to be allowed to watch men in that state was simply wrong, though we were never able to explain in detail to our parents what had been so horrible about the holiday.

That wasn't all that was wrong. Hilliard's wife, Diana,

kept the refrigerator door locked, as well as the pantry. It was, she said, because the servants were thieves. Simon and I were shocked that the food was locked away. Our mother always remembered that she had been hungry when she was a girl, especially when her father had been rector of a parish in one of the poorer parts of Port Elizabeth; and one of her absolute principles as a mother was that there should always be available for her children – and in effect that meant for the servants too – a loaf of bread and a pot of jam; there might not always be butter, but there was always bread and jam. When we went away, she put into our luggage a packet of biscuits and a bar of chocolate: 'for emergencies', she would say.

The emergency happened quickly that holiday. We were too far from the town to replace the biscuits and the chocolate; fortunately, there was a *smous* (itinerant pedlar) who had set up stall near the Witwatersrand Native Labour Association (WNLA) recruiting centre, and he sold us biltong, boiled sweets and hard chocolate, which we ate carefully when our cousins weren't watching. There was almost nothing to do: we didn't have our bicycles with us, and Adrian and his sister didn't offer to lend us theirs; there was no library; there weren't as many books in the house as we were used to having; there were some dams nearby, newly made, but most of them looked unhealthily full of chemicals. Adrian spent his time making a very complicated board game and while we quite liked Gail she was at an age when she didn't have much time to spare for two male cousins. There were two collie dogs, but they had uncertain tempers, and Simon was scared of large dogs, because he had been attacked once before; at first, we used to take them for walks, but one day one of the collies decided to go for Simon – I guess it sensed his fear – and, while Simon ran yelling round and round me, the dog pursued him, until I managed to make Simon stop, so that I could stand between him and the dog to make it quieten down. There were no more walks with dogs – not that they had been much fun, in that bleakly flat landscape.

Simon developed a very painful bladder infection; he kept feeling he wanted to wee but, when he went, nothing happened. To my astonishment, I heard Hilliard's wife telling mother on the telephone that the cause was that I bullied Simon. Simon knew it wasn't; so did I. The water from the taps tasted bad; we couldn't get into the fridge to get iced water; there was no fruit juice – but, most of all, we were bored, lonely and confined.

Fortunately, my mother's old friend from the Kroonstad days, Phyllis Moll, mother of my friend Peter who had drowned so tragically on the family farm, came to our rescue. My mother had telephoned her that we didn't seem to be very happy, so she drove over to collect us, ostensibly for a weekend. Being on the Molls' farm again after so many years was wonderful and we overflowed with food and drink. Simon's urinary problem disappeared overnight. Old Piet Moll showed us the farm and let us fire a Colt 45 through a metal bar; he lent me a .22 rifle and I shot a dove, but then decided I would shoot only at targets. We explored the farm on our own and were driven into Kroonstad to see the rectory where we had once lived; the two fir trees which had been planted in the back yard to celebrate our births were enormous now. Before the weekend was out, we had persuaded Phyllis Moll to arrange for us to see out our holiday with her, rather than return to the Hilliard Drivers. A few happy days later, Piet and she put us on the train to Grahamstown, and what we had left behind in Welkom came with Adrian when he returned to St Andrews for the start of the new term.

We saw Hilliard once again, eleven or twelve years later, at our father's funeral. Before the service started, I turned round in the pew in which my mother, Simon, Dorothy, Astley and I were sitting to see how full the cathedral was – and there he was, so like my father to look at, that for one tiny moment I thought it actually was my father there, and that the whole nightmare of his death and funeral was some sort of ghastly mistake; then I realised it was in fact Hilliard, and I was sorry we hadn't made better friends when we had had the chance, though I don't suppose he was very happy that his cousin's son was so involved in anti-apartheid politics. Certainly, he didn't stay to talk to Simon and me at the end of the service. I suspect too that the 'A. Driver' who wrote letters to the newspapers in Natal supporting apartheid, often just after I had been in the newspapers myself for speaking out against it, was my strange cousin, Adrian.

******

Now that I know more about schools than I did then, I realise St Andrew's College in those days was not (by most objective standards) a very good example. There were some clever boys in the school, as their subsequent careers showed; but the academic results were simply not as good as they should have been. Prowess in games mattered more than anything else – and team games were what showed one's character (not singing in the choir, nor playing in the orchestra, nor taking a role in a school play). Lip-service was paid to the notion that the Chapel was the centre of life at school; but actually the moral centre of the school was on the main games field, 'Lower', where the 1st XV and the 1st XI performed. Ask any boy of my generation what mattered more, a first-class matriculation certificate or colours for rugby, and the answer would have been unequivocal. There were some good teachers – in an intellectual sense – and I was lucky enough to come across three of them: but too many of the teachers merely repeated themselves, year after year, sometimes dictating to us notes which they had dictated to our fathers (we knew this for a fact, as one boy had the notes for Chemistry his father had taken, and they were identical to what we were being told to write down thirty years later).

Because Simon and I had grown up with them and because they were people who had worked with my father, I knew many of the teachers well, and indeed loved some of them; but too many were 'characters' rather than 'teachers'. As such they had a kind of value; but now (especially when I meet people of my own age who were at the better English schools) I wish I had learned more at school. I feel disloyal even as I write this; my father got his education there entirely free (because his father was an Old Andrean killed on active service) and my brothers and I got ours for a small percentage of the real costs (because our father was a clergyman). I was very lucky; I know their names will mean nothing to those they didn't teach, but I name them to honour their memory: Marjorie McKerron, English; Mike de Lisle, Latin; and Peter Harvey, Maths. I made the most of that, and at university had more good fortune in my teachers; but for someone like Simon – and indeed in due course our little brother Astley – what St Andrew's offered in those days was inadequate.

The only man on the staff I came to dislike intensely was Eric Norton. Because he was one of the very few men (perhaps the only man) who had played both rugby and cricket for the country, he was regarded in white South Africa as a heroic figure. Although we were obscure cousins (it was difficult for white families settled in the Eastern Cape not to be related in some way), there was bad blood between the Nortons and Drivers, going back it seemed several generations. I have no idea what the original cause had been, but it extended to relations between my grandfather Gould, when he was a curate of Grahamstown Cathedral, and an earlier generation of Nortons. More recently, there had been a considerable falling-out between my father and Eric Norton over the selection of a Rhodes Scholar.

St Andrew's is one of the schools in South Africa to which Cecil John Rhodes in his will had given its own scholarship to take a pupil each year to Oxford. Our father had been the St Andrew's Rhodes Scholar in 1932, and as a consequence was secretary of the selection committee during the time he spent teaching at St Andrew's. One year, there were two front-running candidates: W.D.C. ('Bill') Chalmers, whom our father thought by a long way the most brilliant boy he had ever taught; and Peter van der Merwe, Head of Upper House in my time, Head of School, Captain of Cricket, and in due course captain of the South African national X1. My father backed Chalmers; Norton – and many others – backed Van der Merwe. Chalmers won; and Norton never forgave my father. In later years, and especially when Chalmers came down from Oxford without taking his degree and Van der Merwe achieved first national and then international fame as a cricketer and a leader of cricket teams, my father would confess that he was by no means so sure any longer of the rightness of his decision to throw his considerable weight behind Chalmers' candidature. I must record the fact that Peter van der Merwe, whom I liked and admired at school and then at the University of Cape Town, never held my father's backing of Chalmers against me personally. I should also record, I guess, that Bill Chalmers worked for my father at Uplands School when he came down from Oxford, and in due course married the matron, who just happened to be the younger daughter of my housemaster from St Andrews; in due course, too, after his time as a schoolmaster, Bill Chalmers achieved the odd distinction of becoming Head of Religious Broadcasting for the South African Broadcasting Corporation (SABC) in the days of apartheid.

One of my refuges from the boredom of most of my lessons became the taking of prep (what would have been called 'homework' in a day school) in the house. Most of the other prefects had work to get on with, and they wanted to do it in the peace of their studies. I ended up taking not only my own allocation of prep duties, but anyone else's who cared to hand it over. Instead of attending to my own work, I would wander around the prep room, helping younger boys with their work; I had done some teaching already at Uplands, and it gave me real joy to see understanding grow as I helped with some mathematical puzzle or unravelled a Latin sentence. Indeed, I would often end up with three boys sitting at my prefect's dais, and I would teach them there.

It was this that led to my big falling-out with Eric Norton. I sat one evening, after prep had officially ended, with three boys at my desk, struggling to help them complete some work Norton had set. The boys were Simon and his two closest friends; they found Maths a particular trial but, that evening, after much prodding and rubbing-out and rough work, they seemed to catch on. The work was right; and they understood why it was right. Next day, they handed their work in, for once confident. Eric marked it, frowning: all three had full marks. 'You cheated,' he told them.

'No sir,' one of them replied. 'Big Driver helped us during prep.'

'I told you not to get help; I told you to do it on your own.'

'No sir, you didn't.' That would almost certainly have been my brother's voice; he was never very good at school subjects, but he had as clear a sense of the difference between right and wrong as anyone I have ever met, and a loathing of injustice as pronounced as his red hair. If he had been told not to get help, he wouldn't have or, if he had, he would have admitted to cheating without demur.

'I told you not to get help,' Mr Norton said. 'Go to your housemaster tomorrow morning.'

'Go to your housemaster' meant one thing only: go to be beaten. The three boys came to see me, distressed not so much at the impending punishment – though at least one of them was the kind of boy for whom a beating was actually worse than just the physical – but at what they thought injustice. So, the next morning, the four of us presented ourselves to the housemaster. 'Mr Norton has sent the three of them to be beaten for cheating, sir; but if you beat them, I think I should be beaten too, because if they cheated I helped them.'

I know perfectly well that it was an article of his housemaster's faith that he did not beat his prefects. He might demote a prefect and then beat him, but there was between him and his prefects a bond of trust which corporal punishment would demean. He got the full story from the four of us, checking the facts quietly. 'Well,' he said, 'ur, ur, I shall talk to Mr Norton at break,' he said. 'You'd better ur, ur, come back to see me ur, ur, after lunch.'

After lunch, we duly presented ourselves. Our housemaster was clearly in a sombre mood, and (as always when he was under strain) his stutter was even more severe than usual, but quickly he told Simon and his friends that they were free to go. To me, he said, quietly, 'Well, ur, ur, I've decided, ur, ur, in the circumstances, that I can't punish them and I ur, ur, have no intention of punishing you. You can ur, ur, go now, though ur, ur, I'm not sure ur, ur, you will thank me for the ur, ur, decision.'

'Thank you, sir.' If I sounded triumphant, it was because I hadn't then quite understood his last sentence.

The next day, when the Sixth Form Maths set trooped in for our lesson, Eric Norton launched into a tirade, not against me by name, but against the 'Upper House prefects'; there were two other Upper House prefects in the class, though neither had had anything to do with the incident. I would have told my study mates, but probably no one else. I can't remember now what the exact terms of the attack were, but they were delivered with a virulence which shocked even those boys who knew nothing about what had happened. Certainly, the head of school, Kennedy Maxwell – a friend from White River – felt so strongly about what Eric Norton had said that he went to the headmaster to protest.

Eric Norton hadn't finished with me, but that is another story. A consolation is that, when he became headmaster of the school a few years later, he was soon regarded as a disaster – the worst headmaster the school had ever had, a knowledgeable friend told me.

I mustn't pretend that my own years at St Andrew's were entirely unhappy, though I ended my time there so bored that leaving was a joy. In many ways I was much happier there than I had been at the prep school. For Simon, I suspect that boarding school was almost entirely a misery, although he did have a capacity for pushing the miserable to one side of his life so that he could get on with living.

******

In a way, not enjoying boarding school was made worse by the fact that the move to White River turned out to be a kind of flowering, especially as it happened just when we were both beginning to grow up. At the start of our first holiday at Uplands, mother announced that we had been invited to a square-dance party. 'We don't want to go,' Simon and I chorused. I had never been very keen on parties, even birthday parties: I loathed the singing of 'Happy Birthday', thinking it an ugly tune, and it was banned at my parties. We both loathed jelly, which always seemed slightly alive to us. We had never been the kind of family which played silly party games, charades or anything like that; whenever we were subjected to them at other people's houses, our aim was to get eliminated in the first round, then we would sit to watch other people's being foolish. No, we weren't going square dancing. 'Oh yes you are,' said mother and she clearly meant it. She didn't often put her foot down.

We had a marvellous time. In many ways, square dancing is an ideal activity for young adolescents, if only they can be persuaded to drop their sophistication or their shyness long enough to join in. There is an element of being bossed about: you have to do as you're told, so you can't just squiggle about on your own, pretending to be absorbed. It is very active – you sweat (especially in the Lowveld). There are generally even numbers of boys and girls; and you get to dance with everyone, fat or thin, pretty or ugly, spotty or radiant. You get to touch each other, but not so much as to be embarrassed.

After a year or two, the craze for square dancing passed and we began to move to the more conventional kinds of dancing. Someone organised dancing classes at the Planters' Club, though that was embarrassing because the teacher insisted that, to dance properly, the boy's tummy had to be against the girl's tummy, close enough to hold a record cover there. The problem was that, for boys, below the tummy was something else, often not obedient to the dancing mistress or even its owner; and, for girls, above the tummy there was what they were both proud of and embarrassed about. How on earth does one touch tummies without touching other things too? For me, of course, towering over almost everyone still – though my friends had begun to grow, thank God – if I pressed my tummy forward (not that there was much of it in those days) it would rest against the bosom of my partner. Whatever the teacher said, in public at least I stayed safely apart from my dancing partner, except when the lights were very low.

Fortunately, the advent of jiving saved us from the awkwardness of proper dancing. One still had a partner, and one touched hands, and occasionally put a hand on the girl's waist; and jiving was at least as vigorous as square dancing, probably more so, because there was no respite while the music was playing. There was also the South African version of the jive, the *kwela*, with the insistent and high-pitched shriek of the penny whistle to get, and keep, one going. Though I was never capable of some of the gymnastic embellishments of my more athletic friends, I had enough sense of rhythm to manage even rapid jiving and being very tall was for once an advantage, because I could twirl my partner safely under one hand; some of our smaller friends, dancing with buxom girls, could find themselves being pushed right off the dance floor if the girls got too vigorous.

As far as the young were concerned, the main activity at the Planters' Club was tennis, rather than dancing, although the underlying purpose was still the same: to meet as many girls – and boys – as possible. As far as I can remember, we would go there two or three afternoons a week, to play on the several courts available to us. We mostly played mixed tennis, rather than the serious stuff – though, of course, this being South Africa, there were some fiercely competitive matches, especially those played by men's or even boys' fours. Similarly, the hockey played on the gravel pitch in the centre of White River (which served both cricket and hockey) was mixed, though no less ferocious for that reason. We enjoyed the tennis, and played the hockey because it was a way of meeting friends; I found that the least active position on the hockey field was left wing in the forward line (playing back tended to involve heavy encounters with more skilled players – sensible players soon learned not to pass the ball to me, on the wing up front and on the left). I could lean on my stick and chat to the girls in their short skirts, while the rest of the players rushed about madly. Simon, being even less of a games player than his big brother, stayed safely on the sidelines.

There was a lively crowd of young, mainly English-speaking, boys and girls to be friends with. There were tennis parties and dancing parties. There were picnics and swimming parties. There were *braai-vleises* (the South African version of barbecues) and expeditions to Bushman's Rock or into the Kruger National Park. The Driver family had much less money than most of the families whose children we went around with; but we had the school, and the school had a pool, and a tennis court, and a playing field, and dormitories where friends could stay overnight, and a hall big enough for dances. So what if we couldn't afford to hire a band to play for our dances, as some of our richer friends did, and we had to make do with records and a record player controlled by a friendly father; but – when I compare the way Simon and I lived in those days with the way our English contemporaries lived – it is usually the children of ducal estates I find myself most in tune with.

And then it was back to school: a night on the train to Johannesburg; a day in the metropolis, sometimes with our father's sister, Kathleen Leith, or with a school friend of his, or with one of our own friends; then a night, a day, and another night on the long journey southwards through the Free State and the Karoo, a change of trains at Alicedale, and the slow slow ride through the hills and into Grahamstown. School was school, to be endured until it was time to go back home, to parents, to little sister and brother, to what I think we knew even then was a temporary heaven.

******

After Simon had failed his matric so hopelessly that it was clear there was no point in his trying to take it again, my parents and he decided he should consider becoming a farmer; not of animals – he would never have been able to kill anything he had nurtured – but for most of his childhood he had had a small garden in which he grew succulents and rock-plants, so some sort of training in horticulture might be sensible. Before the parents undertook the expense of a full-time course at an agricultural college, they decided he should have some experience on a farm. Through the good offices of a wealthy family friend, who owned several farms near them in the Lowveld, they arranged for Simon to spend a year living and working on a farm down the valley from us – a farm devoted in part to citrus fruits, but also to dairy cattle. The manager was given the task of introducing Simon to what farming would involve.

What kind of man this manager (I can't remember his name) turned out to be is perhaps best revealed by something which in fact happened a year or two later. He and his family regularly attended the small Anglican church nearby, where my father doubled up the work he already did as a headmaster by acting as vicar. Among the communicants in the small congregation were the members of an Indian family who ran a shop in the area. It was the only church they could have attended, and it was quite clear from the way they behaved that they were there not to make any kind of political point, but for purely religious reasons: they were quiet, self-effacing, anxious to give no offence, sitting always in the back pew. The farm manager went to see my father to tell him he must instruct the Indians to go to their own church. 'This is their own church,' my father explained. 'They are Anglicans, just like you and me.'

'They are Indian. They should go to their own church.'

Very gently, my father said, 'You know, there is no apartheid in heaven.'

'How do you know?' came the fierce reply. As my father said when he told me the story, there is no answer to that. The family found themselves another church – and the Indians went on quietly attending, with no objection from anyone else, or at least no stated objection that my father heard.

The same man, given the task of introducing my gentle brother to the pains and pleasures of farming in South Africa in 1960, did so in such a way that very soon Simon had what amounted to a breakdown. I don't think even my parents got the full story – and it was years before Simon told me some of what had happened. He had been given every foul job the farmer could think of, especially those involving dealings with the nether regions of animals, and including what I think is called 'drenching' a cow. According to my brother, this involved pushing a hose-pipe up a cow's vagina – and, when the hose couldn't be got in, Simon was made by the farm manager to push his own arm up the cow as far as he could, for no particular purpose other than to 'break him in' to the realities of farming.

That wasn't the final reality of South African farming in those days. According to my brother, the manager claimed to have caught one of his black workers stealing; the police were not called, but the worker was shut in a barn, and there he beat him with a *sjambok* (leather whip). After a time, he handed the *sjambok* to my brother, and told him to continue the beating. My brother refused, and took himself home to my parents. He was, he said, never going to set foot on a South African farm again. I was away at the university by then, and never got the full details of the bullying, and of Simon's breakdown – but I know it was physical as much as nervous. When Simon was under strain, he got boils – in armpit or groin, more like carbuncles than merely boils.

******

The rest of that year Simon spent doing what he could to help at home, putting together a portfolio of drawings and paintings, and recovering his health. Then, despite his lack of academic qualifications, he managed to get a place at art college in Johannesburg, to take a diploma in commercial art. He lived in the YMCA and took himself daily to the college. The family was struggling financially: although I had various bursaries and scholarships to keep me at the university, I was partly dependent on an allowance from home; Dorothy and Astley were still at school. When Simon could, he went home to my parents for weekends, and always for his holidays, or he joined the family when they went to Durban to see a great-aunt or to what was then Lourenco Marques in Portuguese East Africa, where my father did 'locums' for the Anglican priest.

I would see Simon at the YMCA in Johannesburg when I passed through, and at home during the holidays. I still have two of the paintings he did in those years as a student: a ghostly painting of two horses' skulls superimposed on each other and an even more extraordinary painting of a sombre group of miners, black and white, huddled together as if trapped in a mine shaft or in the cage of a mine lift. I thought then, and still think now, that he had the potential to be an extraordinary painter, but he was determined to put his talents to commercial use: he wanted to make money – art would have to come second. So his first task was to learn to draw. Dorothy remembers his making, in those years, dozens of meticulous drawings of cameras.

With the diploma safely achieved, he took a post with a commercial art firm in Johannesburg. He lived frugally at the YMCA, and he saved as much of his salary as he could. We didn't discuss politics; we didn't need to, really: we had the same opinions about everything which mattered. I can't remember whether he actually joined the Liberal Party, as I did; he may well have been too cautious to commit himself that far – but he loathed apartheid, and thought that white South Africa's treatment of and attitudes towards blacks (including coloured people and Indians) demeaned and diminished not just black people but whites too. Other members of the extended family might worry when I became more involved in political activities; some might even fear for their own safety – but Simon (and indeed Dorothy and Astley, not to mention our mother) were constant supporters. The more I was attacked, the more they would defend.

Our father died suddenly in January 1964, aged fifty-two, a fortnight after leaving Uplands School to take up what was meant to be a temporary, recuperative post as a curate in the cathedral in Bloemfontein. Simon and I had been home for Christmas, though I had left again before the New Year because I was required back in Cape Town. We knew our father was ill – he had had several heart attacks already, and had been on sick leave from the school for some time in 1963 – but we assumed he would recover once the strain of headmastering was removed.

Simon and I had had our usual happy time in the Lowveld; the family's impending departure was a complication, of course, because we didn't know when we would be back again, but there was no sense that our departure was to be as final as it turned out. We had our circle of old and new friends and – although some of the parents disapproved of my political opinions and activities, which were already being reported in the national press – the patterns of our partying were too well established to be much disturbed by a young man's odd views.

So we met in town in the morning, played tennis or went riding and swam in the afternoon, then dressed up – the boys in dinner jackets or smart blazers, the older girls in their strapless dresses and long skirts, the younger ones in party frocks – and danced, to music from long-playing records or (if the hosts were wealthy enough to afford a live band) to African jazz and *kwela* played by the combo that usually played in Gardees' Indian Store on the edge of the town. We then drove home in our parents' cars, making sure that we dropped off last the girls we wanted most.

One of our hostesses – who thought my political views quite mad but merely the product of a temporary wildness – fed Simon and me our champagne, not in glasses but in silver tankards, because that is how her husband (a fighter pilot who had been shot down over Warsaw) and his friends had drunk theirs in the wonderful years before the war destroyed everything. It was after that particular event that Simon and I crept up the back stairs, well after dawn, carrying our shoes;

as we tiptoed down the corridor, we heard our mother saying, 'I'm worried about the boys; I didn't hear them coming in last night.' We managed to get into our beds, still in our clothes but with sheets pulled over our heads, before she arrived to check. 'They must have come in hours ago,' we heard her telling our father. 'They're fast asleep.'

Simon had been searching hard in Johannesburg for a better job than he had landed after he had finished his diploma course. Early in the new year, he found what looked like a promising position. Because the firm didn't need him to start at once he was able to help the family with the move to Bloemfontein. So he was in what was meant to be our new home when our father had his fatal heart attack. Simon sat with him while our mother ran to the Deanery to telephone for an ambulance. He told me – when I arrived next morning having borrowed a friend's car to drive overnight from Cape Town – that it had been horrible to watch someone dying. He had known very quickly the ambulance was going to be too late.

I remember almost nothing about the next few days. The friend who had shared the driving on the overnight journey from Cape Town took the car back. The undertaker wanted me to go to look at my father in his coffin; I had no desire to do so and refused – the person I had known and loved wasn't there any more. This was just his poor damaged body, which we needed to dispose of decently and swiftly.

We didn't think there would be much of a turnout at the funeral in the Cathedral; the family had been in Bloemfontein less than a fortnight when father died. In the event, there were more people there than we expected, partly because the local clergy turned out in force: were there really eleven clergy on show at the service? That's the number in my memory. Bill Burnett, with whom we had shared a house after the war, and by now Bishop of Bloemfontein, officiated and preached a sermon, mainly on the theme of 'the laying on of hands'; I had hoped for something more conventional, which would mention my father's war service and career as a schoolmaster, but my mother seemed to find his words a comfort. I had said to the family before the service what I thought my father would have said to us if he had been there: the Drivers would have the straightest backs in the cathedral. Mother, Dorothy and Astley stayed in the Cathedral while Simon and I followed the coffin to the cemetery. I had asked the undertaker to make sure the grave-diggers didn't start to pile the earth and stones back in until we were out of earshot.

Looking back now, I can see better what the loss of our father meant in practical terms to the family; at the time, the immediacy of grief, and the details of the funeral and burial, choked everything. The family had very little money: although our father had carried insurance policies, he had borrowed as much as he could against them to pay school and university fees – and the repayments he had made from the gifts given him as he was leaving Uplands hadn't reached the insurance company by the time he died, meaning that his cheques were invalid. The pension offered by the Anglican church was so small that it was insulting. There was no pension from the schools he had worked in, and nothing like a national scheme of pensions for teachers. The family owned no house, and there was no housing on offer for the widows of clergy. I was paid a pittance by the National Union of South African Students, and Simon's wages were barely enough for him to live on. The family owned very little, not even a motor car. After the burial, the father of a university friend handed me an envelope containing a cheque for fifty pounds; I handed it to mother, not realising that, in fact, it was the only cash she had.

Simon went back to his job in Johannesburg; I went back to the head office of the National Union of Students in Cape Town; Astley went back to school (when, at the end of the next term, he failed his exams, he was beaten by his housemaster); our mother got a job as matron in the sanatorium of St Andrew's, and Dorothy was allowed to live with her while she attended the university, but on condition she didn't use the boys' entrance – she was required to go to and from the matron's flat by way of the fire escape. It is not surprising that the arrangement lasted only months before our mother and Dorothy rebelled.

Over the next few years, Simon and I watched our mother go back to being the person we must have known when we were babies and she on her own with her husband away at the war. She got a part-time job in a shop, then another as an accountant in a garage; then, thanks in part to a diploma in French she had been awarded as a young woman in the Alliance Francaise in Paris, she was appointed warden of a women's residence at Rhodes University.

******

Simon was much more of a loner than I ever was – and while he had friends he wasn't going to spend money on an unnecessary social life. I don't mean at all that he was what white South Africans call *snoep* – mean, miserly, the kind of person who always finds it necessary to go to the lavatory just before his turn comes to buy the drinks. Simon wasn't like that at all; he just wouldn't put himself in a situation in which he might be expected, or might expect of himself, to have to spend money he didn't want to spend. He was determined to save. He wasn't going to be poor all his life; one day he'd be a rich man. To the family he was generous; he would pay his share of the bill if he and friends went out for a meal; he would buy nice presents; and, later, when he began to have some money, he was happy to spend it to buy something beautiful which he really wanted. He just hated to waste money.

He was always a collector. As a small boy, he had collected succulent plants to grow in a rockery. My mother's brothers – the two who had been killed up north – had collected stamps. I was given Uncle Charles's album, Simon Uncle Astley's. I collected a few stamps in a desultory way to add to Charles's collection, but then got bored and, in due course, handed the collection over to Simon. All his life, he added to both collections. One of the few requests he made before his death was to ask our mother to keep up the collection of first-day covers of South African stamps.

As children, we had played with lead models of farm animals and soldiers, making farmyards and battlegrounds in sandpits or on bedroom floors. Simon turned our childhood pastime into a lifelong passion: he collected farm animals, safari animals, lead soldiers, a model of the Coronation coach, an English fox-hunt and more. When he died, they were given to me, and I was supposed to sell them; but I can't bring myself to do so. I suppose I live in the hope that, one day, lead models will no longer be thought of as dangerous for children to play with; and then I shall be able to pass them on to the grandchildren. Simon would have liked that.

He collected old pewter too, and was beginning to accumulate old Cape furniture – yellowwood and stinkwood. He would see a piece he liked in a shop somewhere; he would check it carefully; he would get a price; then, if the price seemed reasonable, he would go away to think about it. Often, if he had spotted something good and cheap, it would have gone by the time he went back for a second look. He'd shrug, grin, and begin to look again. He was in no hurry. Better to miss an opportunity than to buy something which he'd come to regret.

He never bought a place of his own, but always stayed in boarding houses or rented flats. Part of the reason for not owning a house or even a flat was that he never married. I suppose I must say something about his sexuality: we never talked much to each other about sex – for instance, neither of us would have dreamed of boasting to the other about a sexual exploit (initially, I wrote 'conquest', but deleted it because Simon would have hated even the idea of anything sexual being a 'conquest'; he probably wouldn't much have liked the idea of 'exploit' either). I remember once being surprised when he showed me a girlie magazine and then pointed out as particularly appealing a photograph of a girl sitting on steps, wearing a long skirt arranged in such a way one could see she wasn't wearing knickers – well, one could see a bit more than just what wasn't there. I had seen many more and much more pornographic images, but I wasn't going to discuss them with my little brother.

Of course, I am writing this without a biographer's usual tools (very few documents, no interviews with people he knew or worked with, merely memories: my own, my wife's, Dorothy's, Astley's, those of family and friends) and we were apart for most of our adult lives: I in England, except for five years in Hong Kong, and prohibited from returning to South Africa, and he in South Africa, able to travel but not wanting to spend too much money on expensive flights. I remember our mother saying to me once that she wondered if most of Simon's relationships would not have been with 'shop-girls'; she wasn't I think being a snob, just specific, though she might have taken a different position if he had actually decided he wanted to marry one. I don't suppose she ever witnessed his flirting with other women in the way he did if he found them attractive, somewhat awkwardly and always only slightly. Her comment shouldn't have surprised me; most of the women Simon would have met either worked in the shops he frequented or in the firms he did business with or in the bars where he drank – and, since he was, for all the oddities of his appearance and manners, an interesting man, when he asked them out – I guess only after careful consideration and in expectation of judicious expenditure – some of them would say yes. I suspect he wouldn't have asked anyone out if he hadn't already had a clear indication that she would say yes. And if she had said no he would not have 'pressed his suit'; he was always inclined to take what people said at face value.

I know very little about the work he did, although he would show me the catalogues he produced with considerable pride in their meticulous detail. There were photographs of models there, of what were often called, coyly, 'Cape girls', some of them in skimpy underwear. I don't think Simon ever took the photographs himself (on his trips to England, he never brought a camera with him), but I think he would have made sure he supervised the shoots, whether they were of bed-linen or crockery or curtains or attractive women; and that may have given him other opportunities to meet women. Because most of his grown-up years were spent in Cape Town, it would surprise me if some of the women he 'went out with' (to use the phrase of the times) weren't what was then called 'coloured' – or at least dark-skinned girls 'passing as white'.

One has to remember – uncomfortable though it may be to do so – that in those years the Immorality Act, which forbade 'mixed marriages' and any sexual contact across the colour bar, was always a danger to respectability, though in the Cape especially it was breached constantly. The main road through the rich suburbs from Newlands to Wynberg was known as 'Immorality Mile' and, on every street corner, indeed under every tree and lamp-post, stood a coloured prostitute. One would see white men in big cars cruising slowly down the road, surveying what was available, then one of the cars would slide round a corner, the back door would open, the woman would climb into the back seat and snuggle down out of sight, and the car would speed off. Of course it was dangerous – sometimes there would be police cars parked further down the road and occasionally someone would be arrested, and even more occasionally there would be a story in the newspapers – but these were risks one could take: these were the days before AIDS.

There was one disastrous relationship which he told Dorothy and me about, though never in any detail and (as far as I was concerned) only very obliquely: some woman who had been made pregnant by another man decided Simon might make an appropriate surrogate father of her child. She pretended to fall in love with him, and persuaded him that he was in love with her. He was not a hard-headed man, for all his caution. Quite why the charade collapsed we don't know: did she lose the baby? Did Simon work out the truth? Did she decide she couldn't go through with the deception? Understandably, he was for some time very depressed as a consequence.

There were happier love affairs, including one with someone who had been at school with Dorothy. She reported to Dorothy that Simon was very nice to go to bed with, though she had worried that he seemed lonely, almost starved of physical affection. He did have one other, more serious relationship that the family knew about, with someone called Mary, an Irish woman working in Cape Town. If we ever knew her surname, we have forgotten it. I never met her, but other members of the immediate family thought well of her, and she was introduced to my mother, who approved. I was told – though not by Simon – that she was beautiful, and a devout Roman Catholic with strict views about pre-marital sex. It seems that Simon was thinking seriously of asking her to marry him, though he was being as cautious as ever. Then, suddenly, he dropped her.

Oddly enough, though I know so little of the woman – indeed could not even remember her Christian name until my wife, Ann, reminded me – I know precisely why Simon dropped her. They were out together somewhere. A mother began breast-feeding her baby in public near them. Mary expressed disgust. And that was it: for Simon, breast-feeding was right, proper, natural. That was what breasts were for; the act of breast–feeding could never be disgusting. Our father and mother would have said exactly the same. How on earth could he propose marriage to someone who thought anything as inhuman as that? Particularly as there may have been in the expression of disgust an element of the racist: the breast-feeding woman was black.

When he was very ill, a few years later, I know he regretted not so much the decision as that he had never explained. He wondered how one might track someone down again, whom one had rejected so totally. He thought she had left Cape Town to go back to Ireland. Then she wrote to him, but without giving an address. He thought the postmark might have been London, but he had no real idea. And it was too late anyway. He should have been married; he liked children, and was very good with nieces and nephews. On one of his visits to us in England, both Ann and I were working very much full-time. He took over the collection of our four year-old daughter from her nursery school each afternoon, and would look after her until Ann came home; they became very close friends, and I noticed on a visit to her home recently that she still has a framed photograph of 'Uncle Simon' displayed on a wall.

******

Simon had first come to England in 1966, while I was a student at Oxford. I went by train to Southampton to meet him off the Union Castle liner which had brought him from Cape Town. I remember his leaning over the side of the liner, looking down to where I stood on the dockside, and shouting, 'Eh man, brother, you're so white; doesn't the sun shine here?' Although he spent some time in Oxford with me, staying in the tiny cottage on Osney Island which two friends and I rented, he needed to be in London so that he could get a job as a commercial artist. I had arranged for him to lodge with South African friends, Neville and Muriel Rubin, who had a flat overlooking the Thames in Richmond. He stayed there for three or four months, occasionally babysitting their first son, Guy.

Very quickly, he found a job as a commercial artist. He explained to the person who took him on that the one job he couldn't do was lettering, because of his left-handedness. So, naturally, the first job his immediate superior gave him involved a great deal of lettering. At the end of the first week, he walked out and didn't go back, not even to collect the wages he was owed for the work he had done. He found another job, and much the same thing happened. So he gave up the idea of finding a permanent job in London, decided he would live as a tourist to eke out his savings for a few months, and then would go home to South Africa.

I guess the truth of the matter was that he didn't like England: he found the weather depressing; he found English reserve unfriendly; he hated being treated in his work as if he were an ignorant novice; he found lodging – even with thoughtful and kindly friends – very difficult, especially because he liked to be independent of other people's domestic arrangements; and of course South Africa was a cheaper place than London – a little money in Cape Town went much further. Perhaps if I had had a home to offer him, he might have stayed longer, may even have settled; but not only was I still at Oxford, I was talking of going abroad somewhere, to Canada, to the USA or to the West Indies.

When he first went back, it was to Johannesburg, because work was more readily available there. Eventually, however, he moved to Cape Town, where he got a job doing some of the artwork for the catalogues of a big mail-order company; he stayed there for the rest of his life, gradually learning new skills and taking more and more responsibility within the firm, until he was entirely responsible for all the mail-order catalogues it produced. Given the size of the country, and the isolation of many communities, mail-order companies in South Africa were quite big businesses, the equivalent of Sears-Roebuck in the USA; and it seemed that the family which owned the company recognised Simon's skill and loyalty and rewarded him with regular increases. Certainly, he was proud of the work he did, and he never stinted with time and effort.

He lived in a boarding house for a while, then in a cheap hotel and later started renting flats. Holidays were spent mainly visiting our mother, who had moved back to Grahamstown after our father's death, though when he started earning more money he began to travel to Europe; he enjoyed being a tourist, visiting

Rome or Paris or London, seeing the sights, walking the streets, drinking in bars, trying when he could to strike up conversations, though he spoke only English and Afrikaans (he was very funny about trying to speak Afrikaans in the Netherlands, and discovering that most Dutch people prefer to speak English). His travels nearly always ended with time spent with my wife, children and me in England, although – to our regret – he never came to visit us during the five years we lived in Hong Kong.

Then, when I was back in England as headmaster of Berkhamsted School in Hertfordshire, there came a letter (not a telephone call, but a letter) to tell me he had been diagnosed with cancer: after months of pain he had taken the dull but constant ache in his right thigh to be examined by his GP. He had been referred to a specialist, who had had him X-rayed and diagnosed a tumour in the bone of his thigh. It was a rare form of cancer, usually seen only in children; how long the tumour had been growing no one could guess, but the only hope of preventing its spread was to amputate the leg at the hip. It might be already too late, Simon said; but by the time I got the letter the leg would already have gone. The firm was being very good to him, he said; when he was well enough, he was going back to work. Fortunately, he had finished work on the latest catalogues before going to the doctor. He would need to have his car adapted so he could drive it one-legged, but he had been told he could have a tin leg fitted as soon as the wound healed (Simon always called it a 'tin leg', never a 'prosthetic'). He planned, too, to come to England to see me and the family.

It is difficult to explain this now, all these years later, but – as I know from other friends who have found themselves in similar situations – there was a sense that the extremities of daily life (such as a death in the family) overtook political scruples. When people ask me, 'Wasn't he uncomfortable living under apartheid?' the answer is instantaneous and abrupt: what kind of person do you think he was? He loathed apartheid; he was – for a white South African of his class and age – wonderfully free of prejudice, but he lived in that particular country. He might have lived elsewhere, but he didn't. However, he was not a joiner; he would have found membership of a political organisation tiresome, and all the inevitable 'politicking' of politics an aspect of the 'fuss' he hated. He had to make do with what he was and where he was. His political attitudes were made clear in the way he treated the black and coloured people he met and dealt with; and, then, when he was fighting cancer and then fighting death, the other battles inevitably seemed less immediately important.

I have tried to explain some of this in a poem called 'Grace & Silence', in the sequence, *Love & Death in Cape Town*; Grace was the domestic servant who looked after his flat, Silence the caretaker of the block of flats. One could work out a great deal about a person's political views by regarding the ways in which he or she treated people of a different skin colour.

He did, in fact, come twice at this stage to see us in England, once soon after the operation, when we still hoped the cancer hadn't spread beyond its first site, and once after he had had his first bout of chemotherapy. On the second visit, in the spring of 1986, he and I drove to do what we had often talked about but had never got around to, which was to visit the villages around Exmoor that the Gould family had originally come from. Simon had always been much more the family historian than me, and he wanted to see where the Goulds, the Ridds, the Doones, the Tamlyns, the Smyths, and all the rest, familiar from my mother's stories, had lived. It wasn't difficult to find them; every churchyard was replete with gravestones bearing family names, some of which were already in our family records. We had a borrowed wheelchair in the back of the car and, when he was tired of using his crutches, he would allow me to push him through the graveyards and into the churches to see the names of our English family.

Simon had decided that he was going to have one last independent outing in London. He had booked himself into the Piccadilly Hotel for a weekend, and so Ann drove him there. She was very anxious about leaving him at the hotel; the cancer had spread to his lungs, even though the surgeons had excised what they could of the tumours, and he was finding breathing difficult. We had arranged with our GP for him to have a mobile supply of oxygen, though he hated having to use it. Moreover, he hadn't ever managed to cope with the discomfort of the tin leg strapped to his hips, and he relied on crutches or – when he got tired – on a wheelchair; but he was determined to stay in London. I had thought he might be planning one last fling, although my Ann is certain that what he hoped for was a chance encounter with Mary. When she left, he insisted on coming on his crutches to wave goodbye to her from the front of the hotel. A one-way traffic system meant it took her nearly ten minutes to drive past the entrance; but, when she did so, he was still standing there, one-legged on his crutches, ready to wave.

Very quickly, he found that he couldn't cope. Crutches in Cape Town might be enough to get him around; in London they didn't suffice. There was no one to manage a wheelchair for him. Moreover, lugging oxygen canisters around was impossible. Whatever liveliness he had planned to get up to simply wasn't going to be possible, nor was a meeting with Mary ever anything but a dream. I was out of the house, busy with some headmasterly duty, when he telephoned early next morning to ask Ann to fetch him. It was a bad moment, certainly the worst we ever had with him. By the time Ann reached him, he was as close as he ever got to despair.

That evening, he said, quietly, that he wanted me to come back to South Africa to visit him.

******

This was, in fact, much more tricky than it might seem. When my passport had expired in England in 1966, the South African authorities had refused to renew it. Although they had offered me a re-entry permit, it was clear both that no airline would accept me on a flight home for fear I wouldn't actually be allowed into the country, and that the kind of welcome which might await me might be less than cordial. So, after a few years of statelessness, I had become a British citizen. I had then apparently been informed in a letter from the South African authorities that, unlike most other British citizens, I was not regarded as exempt from the requirement to have a visa before I visited South Africa. It was an administratively convenient way of making me a prohibited immigrant in my home country. I had never actually got the letter, though (acting on advice from Helen Suzman, the one Progressive Party MP in South Africa, that I should on no account risk coming back without a visa) I had applied for – and had been refused – one in the late 1970s, when I was doing the research for a biography of Patrick Duncan.

If I applied for a visa, I knew it would either be refused

or, at the least, so delayed that it would come too late. A friend who had applied for a visa to attend his father's funeral had had his request refused. So I decided to take the risk of going without one. Although much of my fifth novel, *Shades of Darkness*, is only very obliquely autobiographical, the section set in the Johannesburg airport is very directly so. I was held for eight hours while the truth of my story was checked; moreover, my file apparently had a note appended that I must not be admitted to the country except with the personal permission of the minister of state concerned – and finding a sufficiently senior official on a Saturday wasn't easy. Eventually, thanks mainly to one good-hearted immigration official, I got my entry visa, though only for twenty-four hours. The next day, when I was in Cape Town with my brother, we managed to get the visa extended.

It was a strange fortnight, mainly with Simon, though Dorothy was living in Cape Town too, and our mother flew from Grahamstown to be with us for part of the time. Dorothy and Simon had become very close, trying always to go out to a restaurant together every week, and often sharing meals at home with each other or with mutual friends. She gave him a great deal of her time, especially after he became ill, even though she was busy with her work at the university.

Because Simon was still insisting on going to work almost every day, I had time to see other friends, although I managed to persuade him to take enough time off to enable us to do some of the more touristy things available in the Cape. At his request, I went with him to see his oncologist. Simon knew that he was dying, but he asked me to ask the doctor on his behalf if she could ensure that he would die without pain; during one of his stays in hospital he had heard a patient with spinal cancer screaming – it was worse because the man in such ghastly pain, which even the strongest drugs couldn't contain, was someone we had known years before when he was Dean of the Cathedral in Grahamstown. I have given some of the detail of that time in the sequence of poems, *Love & Death in Cape Town*.

I think those poems are the best record I can give of those strange weeks; but to give something of the feeling of Simon's quality in those last months let me tell this story. He had run out of reading material, so took himself off to a bookshop in Claremont. He parked his car, struggled on his crutches up the escalator, and was stomping around searching for a novel he might enjoy. He was by that stage very strange-looking: the hair that had re-grown after the chemotherapy was a fluff of pinkish white which was too soft and fine to cut even if he could have been bothered; his pallor accentuated his freckles, which looked more like blotches; he was breathless and panted easily; and of course he was one-legged. Two old women had observed him and, as apparently happens, assumed that as well as being ill my brother was deaf and probably brain-damaged. 'I wonder what's wrong with him,' wondered one.

'Doesn't he look ill?'

'Yes, his skin looks so bad.'

'Oooh, doesn't he look bad with those blotches? And that funny hair?'

'I wonder what he's got,' and so on.

Eventually, Simon could bear their scrutiny and comments no longer. Abandoning his search for something to read, he made to leave the shop. Just as he got to the exit, he paused, turned to look at them, then said, very clearly and crisply, 'It's mange.'

He was still giggling about the incident when he got back to his flat to tell me the story.

I had to leave. We had always found goodbyes difficult and remembered especially the partings from our parents at the Nelspruit railway station, when we would all stand making awkward and desultory small-talk on the platform while we waited for the signal that it was time for us to board the train on our long journey back to school; there was a danger that our mother would start weeping. So, now in Cape Town,

Dorothy, Simon and I went to a restaurant he liked, ate what we could for lunch and then drove to the airport. There seemed nothing else to say; we knew that this was the last time Simon and I would see each other. I hugged Dorothy, then shook hands with Simon, and we said our usual, 'Well, goodbye, brother', before I turned my back to walk away.

His dying took longer than any of us had been led to expect: months, rather than weeks. Ann – by training an occupational therapist and then employed in a hospice in Berkhamsted – had persuaded Simon on his last visit to England that he should take up drawing again, and had supplied him with sketch pads and pencils. He made dozens of meticulous drawings in those last months, most of them intricate studies of plants, the more complicated the better; I imagine that the complexity of the drawings in some way reflected what he felt about the inexorable growth of the cells inside him.

When he became too ill to stay in the flat, even with help, his doctor moved him into a private ward at Groote Schuur hospital. Our mother was summoned from Grahamstown and came down with her new husband (she had re-married after twenty years of widowhood). He enjoyed their visit and seemed to rally, though what he really wanted was to talk to his mother on her own, without her husband listening in (we were fond enough of him, though weren't keen to call him our step-father, despite being grateful that he was – and that he would be – there to look after our mother in her old age). As they were leaving after each visit, Simon would call mother back, often giving some trivial reason, hoping to have a few moments with her on her own; always the husband would come back too, kindly and solicitous, but intrusive.

Simon was permanently on oxygen now, with a mask over his mouth and nose; but, as the doctor had promised, there was no pain, at least as far as our mother and sister could tell. Still, he clung on to what life he had left, and he worked away at the elaborate drawings. Mother flew down from Grahamstown again, this time on her own; still Simon survived, though he was very weak. After a week, she began to get anxious about having been away so long, and her husband was nagging her to return. Simon told her that he thought she really should go home; he wasn't going to die yet. So she went.

Dorothy is convinced he sent mother away quite deliberately; he was ready to die and he didn't want to die alone, but he didn't want her around to make a fuss when it was happening. The nurses had moved a spare bed into his room so Dorothy could sleep there. She is quite sure that, in some way, Simon's actual death involved an act of will. She told me the first time we met afterwards that, as soon as mother had gone, he had set himself to die; that he had behaved like someone about to dive under water: he took the longest breath he could manage, shut his eyes, and quickly slipped into unconsciousness. She stayed the night on the spare bed so she could be with him, but he didn't die. She had to teach that day, and in the evening went back to the hospital to spend another night.

During the night the nurse woke her to say that she thought Simon was very close to death. While the nurse rubbed Simon's ankles and feet – she said dying people always seemed to have cold feet – Dorothy half-lay, half-sat on the bed next to him, stroking his forehead, from nose to hairline, over and over again, whispering to him. She felt that somehow she was helping to ease his soul out of his body. After a while, the nurse told her she could stop; Simon had died.

He had long since abandoned the Christianity in which we had been brought up, but had struck up an acquaintance with a clergyman who visited the hospital and who in the last weeks came daily to talk to Simon in his room. After our mother had come back from Grahamstown, Simon's body was cremated, and the priest buried the ashes, in a simple ceremony attended by a few friends – some of them from his workplace – and family, in a churchyard. The money Simon had so carefully saved was split three ways between Dorothy, Astley, and me; and (as Simon had asked her to do) Dorothy sorted out the possessions, consulted the family, and gave each of us an equitable share, to do with what we willed.

There was one strange episode which I shall recount as a kind of sequel. That there are rational explanations I don't doubt; and I have never been inclined to believe in telepathy or spiritual migration or anything so untested by science, so unproven; nor indeed that we have souls independent of our minds and bodies; yet at the time it was a comfort in my lonely grieving. During those last weeks of his dying, I was in India, on a scheme funded by the Commonwealth Trust to enable me to shadow an Indian headmaster for a few months.

I knew Simon was dying, and he was often in my dreams. One night in New Delhi, I had an extraordinarily vivid dream that he had come to my bedside and had said, in his usual rather gruff and matter-of-fact way, 'Oh, so this is where you are. I've been looking for you. I wanted to tell you that I'm off now. Goodbye'. I woke then, certain that he had died. It was such a detailed dream, so realistic, so convincing, that I thought I really should wake the friends in whose house I was staying so that they could be a kind of witness of the experience; but then I looked at my watch, saw we were in the small hours, so of course didn't wake them.

The next morning, just before breakfast, Ann telephoned from England: Dorothy had telephoned from Cape Town to tell her that Simon had died. She didn't have a telephone number for me in India. When I worked out the time differentials, it seemed to me his dying and my dream must have happened at more or less the same time.

Love & Death in Cape Town

i. Don't Fuss

'The doctors have told me,' my brother wrote,
'There is little else they can do for me –
So I shall accept your invitation
(If I may)' – and so he came to visit,
Kom kuier, in the language of childhood
We still use, because it's our own country
Where I have made a very private peace,
Though only for dying. One-legged, breathless,
As bald as an old man from the chemo
(Not to mention the cobalt, nor the scars
Where the surgeons had cut the bits they could)
He told my children things I'd forgotten
Entirely, but remembered as he told,
Like meeting someone after a long time
Who had once been quite familiar:
That I had held a stone in my right hand
So I could turn that way on dismissal
From parade – I've never known left from right –
How I had frowned with such ferocity
That my nickname had been Old Baboon Eyes –
How I'd lined up shoes on a bedroom sill
To fire at the guinea-fowl machine-gunning
In the dawn – oh, so many stories
Of all the years we gave away to time –
And then he'd cough: and cough, and cough, and
  cough

Until we'd hold our breath and look away,
Or offer him a drink, or to call the doc –
And he'd whisper, 'Don't fuss,' and then he'd cough
Until we thought the scars would have to burst.
But we couldn't fuss, because he said so.

Both he and I knew well, but didn't say,
That when our father died, from his bad heart,
His last words as he lay on the sofa
While my brother sat next to him waiting
And could see what was happening but knew
There was nothing he could do, nor doctors,
Nor the ambulance men, nor hospitals,
Nor the priest next door – nothing, nothing to do
But wait – and, waiting, my father whispered
That last invincible chorus to death:
'Don't fuss.'
      And then he said, 'I think you should ...
You know ... come home. They'd let you in, for me,
I think. Come home. I'd like it very much.'

ii. Grace and Silence

I thought his name was Silas: it suited
Since he collected junk of any kind
And stored it where my brother didn't keep
His car: junk of any kind – half a bike;
Old magazines; a broken saw; a lid
Without a pan, a handless clock, a lamp
My brother'd thrown away; broken glasses;
Cheque book stubs; shelves of any size;
All my brother's left-foot shoes. ('I s'pose,'
My brother said, 'there may be someone else
Who's lost the other leg, and needs those shoes –
Ol' Silas would find him.') He packed it up,
The junk I mean, in huge cardboard parcels
And monthly shipped them back, to the homeland,
Victorian dealer, Miser, Silas,
Quaint and kindly ...
                    'But you've got it wrong,'
My brother said. 'His name isn't Silas –
Silence, that's his name – parents called him that,
In hope he might have been, or since he was,
Like Ruth, I guess, or Hope, or Charity.'
Silence collected junk, for which he found
A use. Silence was always there. Silence
Took care. Silence shook hands and said, warmly,
'So you're the big brother, come from England,
Principal, of a high school, Simon said.'
(Not 'my baas', I was pleased to hear –
'I said he couldn't clean my car if he

117

'Baas'ed me,' my brother said, sotto voce.)
'I am very pleased to meet,' Silence said –
And I was very glad I'd left my bags inside.

Grace, on the other hand, came on Tuesdays
To do the ironing, and clean the flat
(Which needed it by then, I tell you man!).
She borrowed next week's wage to pay the school
Her children wouldn't go to, but he kept
A month or two ahead, and then forgot,
Although he said, 'I think she adds it up, and pays
In overtime.' He wasn't sure. 'Who cares?'
He said. 'It's just a kind of grown-up game
Between the three of us. When Silence needs
A bit of *'geld'*, he cleans my car, then says
"I cleaned your car because it needed me" –
It's a kind of local truce we've made,
I guess. I give them what they want, and they
Protect me, for a little time at least.
That's all I need, you see.'
          Grace and Silence:
Grace does the dishes; Silence keeps the door.

iii. Aubade

A pre-recorded priest awoke me
Who stayed in bed and did not climb the stairs
Of the tower I could not quite see there
Somewhere towards the Cape Town end of Mowbray;
And I remembered other dawns I'd heard
All those years before, in this fated town –
And most of all a friend who woke me up
To come to celebrate his first son's birth –
And we heard the muezzin sing, over Wynberg.
The ghosts of all the slaves who'd built the house
Were gathered round. 'Champagne for sons,' we said,
And 'Freedom in our time.' The old house cheered.

That son's a scion of the further Left
In London now; his father somewhere else
High-up now, one hears; and I am teaching
Clever boys in Berkhamsted. We've grown up –
And some of us have grown away, and some
Are dead, and some will die, and soon, I fear.
The dawn-song blares; the curtains pulse with wind;
The shutters bar the early light. How strange,
How strange it is to be alive, and back
Where I belonged so much, now not at all.

iv. Recognition

I did, I confess, grow sometimes weary:
Dying takes so long, so many trunk calls
And cheerful letters, so many alarms
And long waiting, old *Outspans* and *Digests*
In antiseptic waiting-rooms, aglow
With brave aftershave and nurses rustling.
In the Cancer Outpatients, Kronald's 'firm',
Where I wheeled you, for once in a chair
Though you kept the crutches close, since you could,
If you needed to, walk on your own – 'hell,
I've only lost a leg, not all my brain' –
We saw the old white-haired Congress man, come
(I guess) for a check-up or an X-ray,
Or was it a diagnosis of death?
Grizzled and fit, in charge of his body,
In the way you sometimes get disciplined
In a cell, with certainty of triumph,
And structured hours of careful exercise,
He sat waiting, as he was now used to,
With a fat white warder, spinnaker guts
And a *bokbaard* not quite hiding the chin –
And the shirt-sleeved man with a holster gun
Under his armpit, by the eyes SB
If cold counts any more, who looked at me
As if he half-remembered who I was –
As I did him, all right, standing in my cell
To say, 'We'll get you bastards, every one ...'

And now he slightly frowned, and I wondered
If he wondered what I was doing there ...
And the old black man stared me through as if ...
As if I was just another white man
Waiting for death, in J7, Groote Schuur.

v. Marginal Miranda

Last time I saw Miranda was in Kings –
The inner quad where dwell the dons – but she,
Poor girl, was fat: the spuds had done her in
And filled her out, not merely plump – dumpling:
A suet girl, as fat as Cambridge pie.

I'd known her twenty years; she used to pass
For white, a tiny, silken, dark-eyed dart
(Treble-twenty!). Though it did not touch her brain
To see her fat was just a little sad,
Even in Cambridge, and even in Kings,
Though it's some way to go from District Six.
Now, in Cape Town, I had to ask her name:
'Is that ...?'
        'Yes, it is,' my sister said,
And my brother said, 'Too thin,' reproving.
'She came back?' I asked, amazed. She came back.
Heads were shaken. It was England, or cold,
Or breakdown, or the usual masculine
Antic, something like that. I heard her say
To a man who'd trapped her in a corner,
'Yes, I'm a librarian', and she added –
Like a huge brass name-plate – 'from Grassy Park'.
Coloureds live in Grassy Park, never whites;
You cannot pass for white in Grassy Park.
So coming back was more than just a change
Of scene or style. She had moved centre-page,
Marginal Miranda. She was what she was;

She did not merely seem. I didn't see
Who drove her home, so asked; my brother said,
'She went by 'bus, early; she always does.'

vi. Old Friend

(for Maeder Osler)

And after twenty years apart, old friend –
Best friend, best man, and my best defender
In those bad days of nineteen-sixty-four
(My father dead, my girl-friend gone, and half
My friends in gaol, or run away abroad) –
How good it is to find you now at last
Restored to where you started from, and set
On rich well-watered land, between *koppies*.
May droughts stay well away from all your lands,
Guerrilla fighters not descend this route
From north to south; and may your broad shoulders
Not carry more than proper for a man
Who never tried to shirk the heaped-up guilt
Of all those generations buried there
Below the copse. We fought well in those days,
But now our choices hardly multiply.
We live with what we are, the one choice left
To leave or not: I did, and you did not.
What else to say? Across a brandy bottle
Empty now, you raise an empty glass
And grin at me: 'Eh, man, I tell you what –
Twenty years is but a blink of the eye.'

vii. The Advocaat

Fiction couldn't bear him: he is too odd
To be easily believed in – a Buddhist
And not merely a monk but an abbot
And in California, now returned
To the fatherland because he desires
Possessions: a suit or two, a small house,
A wife and some children. So in chambers
Next to the Hanging Court of the Eastern Cape
He holds temporary sway, and defends
Scarred revolutionaries and scared children.
Who was it made the pattern? Who broke it?
There are different roads to the one river.

viii. The Man Outside the Supreme Court

Above the polished shoes the polished gun:
Above the light blue shirt the pale blue eyes.

ix. Well, Goodbye

I'd been skirting it all day, what I'd say
At our last parting, at the aerodrome
(Our joking way of sharing older times
To use the older terms gone out of taste).
Of course we knew. At lunch I said something
Rather feeble about the next summer
(Already I had shifted hemispheres
And meant the summer on the northern side).
Of course we knew. This was to be our last
Goodbye. There would be no more coming back.
We've always hated partings, kept them brief,
Said, 'Well, goodbye', quickly touched, turned and
walked –
And don't look back.
          And don't look back. And that
Was what we did; habit saved us from grief,
At least in public. It'd been just the same
Leaving home for boarding school, the long wait
On the hot platform, parents standing there,
And nothing left to say, not even
Silly things like, 'Now don't forget to write'.
We used to say to them, 'Goodbye and go.
We're on the train, leaving any moment now.
Why wait? Why drag this parting out? We don't
Want to go away – you know. Any moment now
Mom will cry. Please go. Just say goodbye.'

The night he died, before I heard the news,
I woke at three, in a far country, far
Even from England. I had had a dream.
I often dreamed of him, my small brother
With cancer, though never dead. But this time
He was dead. I was sure. I woke in tears.
He'd come to me, as ghost, or something else,
To let me know, with gruff laconic words:
'So this is where you are: in India ...
I thought I'd better let you know. I'm off ...'
And then, as usual, flatly, 'Well, goodbye.'
And I woke up, in grief but also joy,
Since wordless Simon had to go like that –
And going thus meant something else than death;
And I thought: but no one will believe this –
I should wake my hosts to say, 'My brother's dead;
I know he's dead', before they telephone –
But I can't wake them now; it's three o'clock.
I'll tell them when we meet for morning tea.
I forgot of course. One does. The call came
At breakfast time.

Lightning Source UK Ltd.
Milton Keynes UK
UKOW05f0703040514

231092UK00001B/6/P